Getting the Buggers to Behave

this
ier
not
by another

Also available from Continuum:

Sue Cowley: *Starting Teaching*

Angela Thody, Barbara Gray and Derek Bowden: *The Teacher's Survival Guide*

Duncan Grey: *The Internet in School*

Getting the
Buggers to Behave

Sue Cowley

CONTINUUM
London and New York

Continuum

The Tower Building   370 Lexington Avenue
11 York Road   New York
London SE1 7NX   NY 10017-6503

www.continuumbooks.com

First published 2001
Reprinted 2001 (twice)

British Library Cataloguing-in-Publication Data
A catalogue record for this book is available from the British Library.

ISBN 0-8264-4978-6 (paperback)

Typeset by Paston PrePress Ltd, Beccles, Suffolk
Printed and bound in Great Britain by TJ International Ltd, Padstow, Cornwall

Contents

Acknowledgements

Thanks to all the students who helped with the interviews, especially: Mark, Kirsty, Andrew, Mark, Jason, Paula, Roshney, Sarah, Becky, Nicola, Lisa, Jon, Shaun, Nick, Daniel, Craig, Michael, Nina, Grace, Louise and Lisa. Thanks also to all the teachers who have inspired and helped me in my teaching career – you know who you are!

Thanks to Anthony Haynes for having enough faith in me to publish two of my books. And of course, special thanks to Tilak Castellino, who makes it all possible.

Introduction

Behaviour management: if you get it right, your life is easy, you're free to do what you're meant to do, which is of course to teach! With a well-behaved class, teaching is one of the most wonderful jobs in the world. Every day offers you a new and different experience: the chance to see a child discover a fresh concept, to learn something that they never knew before, the opportunity to make a real difference to the lives of your students. As they say, 'nobody forgets a good teacher', but what exactly does being a 'good teacher' mean?

One of the most essential characteristics of a good teacher is surely the ability to manage our students' behaviour, so that we can facilitate their learning, and this is especially so if you work in a school where there are many behaviour problems. We can only spark that crucial desire to learn if we can first get our children to concentrate, to have self-discipline, to behave themselves! Every student in every school deserves the best education we can possibly offer them, and we must find a way to achieve this. Some schools and some students prove to be a real challenge for any teacher; and even in the easiest schools, there are days when you just can't seem to get it right. This book can help by offering you a wealth of practical ideas to try out in your own classroom, to lend you a hand in 'getting the buggers to behave'.

Teachers use a wide variety of different skills in their everyday work. You need to be a specialist at teaching your subject or subjects, and you must also manage the behaviour of your class or classes so that learning can actually take place. To a certain extent, teachers learn how to do this through actually being in the classroom, and as time goes on you find yourself drawing from a wide bank of ideas and experience to help you. There do seem to be some teachers who are naturally good at regulating behaviour, who have an innate ability to engage and 'hold' a class. However, it is also possible to learn how to improve and increase your behaviour management skills, and that is exactly what this book will help you do.

This book is practical, easily accessible and easy to read. No academic theory – just lots of tips, advice and examples to show how the ideas I give really work in practice. I have also included comments and thoughts taken from interviews with students. After all, it is our students who face us day after day in the classroom, and they often perceive the way we treat them, and the reasons for their misbehaviour, in a very different way to us. In addition, the students that I interviewed had very clear ideas (some of them surprising!) about what makes a teacher a good or bad manager of behaviour.

Teachers today are stressed; there is no doubt about it. This stress is caused by many different factors – poor behaviour, excessive workload, a lack of status in contrast to other professions. What I offer you in this book are some ways of minimizing the stress. That is why this book focuses mainly on strategies for the *teacher*, rather than for the *student*. What I am interesting in doing is helping you as a teacher, helping you survive on a day-to-day basis in a difficult and challenging job, and allowing you to enjoy the amazing career you have chosen.

This book gives you advice on behaviour management that is easily accessible and equally easy to apply. After all, how many of us, snowed under with reports to write and lessons to plan, have time to wade through endless theory? There is plenty of information on the basics of behaviour management, plus lots of tips for controlling your classes and ideas for managing the physical aspects of the classroom environment. The ideas and advice given are based on 'common sense' observations and strategies that have worked for me. My hope is that you will find this book a useful reference source in your everyday teaching, one that you can turn to for ideas when you need them, or to find alternative strategies for dealing with the management of your own class or classes.

So, I do hope that this book will help you in getting *your* students to behave. And if we can get it at least partly right, not only will we improve the education of our students on an everyday basis, but we will also be able to thrive and flourish in the job we love.

Part One

In the Beginning . . .

1 Basics of behaviour management

What are the basics?

In this first chapter we're going to take a look at the basics, the initial 'ground rules' of behaviour management. These are the fundamentals, the things that should become intuitive if your teaching style is going to encourage good behaviour on a consistent basis. Although much of what follows may seem self-evident, it is perhaps worth while refreshing your memory on occasions, or looking at this section again to check whether something really basic is going wrong. In reality, many experienced teachers already do these things so automatically that they forget what it is they're actually doing. Most recently qualified teachers will have been taught about these ideas in college, but sometimes it can seem difficult to match all that theory with the reality of being in the classroom. So what do the 'basics' actually mean in practice? Let's take a look and see.

Be definite	'I know what I want.'
Be aware	'I know what will happen if I don't get what I want.'
Be calm and consistent	'I'm always fair and consistent with you.'
Give them structure	'I know where we're going.'
Be positive	'You're doing great!'

Be definite

'I know what I want.'
Being definite in your teaching is all about knowing what your expectations of your students are. Like predators sensing a weakness

in their prey, students seem to be instinctively aware of vulnerability and uncertainty in their teachers. From the moment you walk through the door, you must 'show no fear'. You should be so certain of what you want from your students that there is no room for them to argue, no chance for them to 'step out of line'. And if your students do misbehave, this should be treated with a suitable level of amazement: how *dare* they defy your expectations!

Interestingly, the point about being definite came up frequently in student interviews. The students explained that if a teacher seems uncertain, acts as though they are scared, or tries to not get on the 'wrong side' of their students, students have far less respect for that teacher. Students want certainty from the adult figures in their lives. They want you to create and enforce boundaries that give them a feeling of solidity. This is perhaps particularly true for your most difficult students, who may lack structure in their home lives, and who may test all the adults they meet to see whether they truly care for them.

Of course, there will be situations and schools where, despite your best intentions, the students simply refuse to comply, and I will deal with some more advanced strategies later on in this book. But even with the most difficult students, the following approaches will help you to cope. So what exactly do you need to be definite about? Here are some thoughts and examples that you might find useful, covering two aspects of a lesson that are often when problems occur: at the beginning and end of class. Obviously, you will already have your own methods of doing these things, but it can sometimes refresh your teaching style to try an alternative.

Entering the room

1. How should the students enter the room? For example, do they

   - line up outside and wait for the teacher to invite them in;
   - enter as they arrive if the teacher is in the classroom?

   The first strategy is probably preferable in 'difficult' schools, as it allows the teacher to structure the entry of the class into the room, and it also demonstrates a high level of control to the students. However, if you are likely to have to wait a long time for those arriving late to your lesson, you might want to consider the second possibility.

2. What do the students do once they are inside your classroom? Do they

   - go directly to their seats, get out their books, pencil cases, diaries, etc, and wait for the register to be taken or the lesson to begin;
   - collect any equipment they need and start work immediately?

Although the first suggestion might seem to offer a more 'controlled' start to the lesson, the second option could actually help you to engage a difficult class more quickly. If you are planning some whole class teaching, the first method may suit you better. However, if the class is going to be doing project work, for instance, they could quite easily get started immediately. In addition, this leaves you free to deal with any troublemakers or latecomers. If you are in the unfortunate situation of teaching classes with many badly behaved students in them, then at least this method allows those students who are motivated to get on with their work, rather than listening to you disciplining the class.

The lesson

1. How will the lesson start? Will it be

   - with the register being taken;
   - with homework being collected in;
   - with the teacher explaining the aims of the lesson?

The choice of whether to 'plunge' straight into the lesson, or to deal with administration first, will depend very much on the type of class you are teaching. If you are dealing with a restless bunch of youngsters, it may be counter-productive to demand that they hand their homework in first. If homework has not been done, you will then set up a series of confrontations that might best be avoided.

   Taking the register at the start of each lesson is a habit I've formed (and stuck with) during my teaching career. I have found it to be a very useful way of pulling the students together and setting up definite expectations of the class. However, it really should be done with the class sitting silently, while the teacher calls out the names and the students answer. This will demonstrate your control, and impose a calm and ordered start on the lesson. The problem with this is, you can't get halfway through and then give up because your students won't be quiet. If you do, they will have 'won' at the first hurdle. 'I've started, so I'll finish' must be your maxim!

2. How will the lesson finish?

   - the students are dismissed a few at a time;
   - all the students stand behind their chairs and wait to be dismissed;
   - the class leaves when the bell goes.

The first of these options allows the teacher to keep behind any students who they need to talk to for whatever reason. The second option offers a very controlled ending to the lesson, and in addition the teacher can check the floor for rubbish and also get the chairs pushed in, leaving the classroom looking orderly. At times, however, you will be so relieved that the class are leaving, that you just allow them to go, wiping your brow in relief at the same time!

Be aware

'I know what will happen if I don't get what I want.'
When things do go wrong, as inevitably they will on occasions, you should be fully aware of what you will do to correct the situation. Again, you must be certain of this: behaviour 'X' will lead to sanction 'Y' and so on. The students must be clearly aware of what will happen if they do choose to misbehave. There is more information on using sanctions in Chapter 5, but let's look briefly now at how you might deal with a student who refuses to do what you want.

If a student does challenge your expectations, try taking the following steps:

- Be *definite* about what you want (and stick to it!).
- Remain calm at all times.
- Stay polite at all times (however difficult this is!).
- State your expectations clearly.
- Clarify any possible misunderstandings.
- State how the student's behaviour is not meeting your expectations.
- State what will happen if they continue to defy you.
- Depersonalize the sanction, by making it clear that the student is forcing you to punish them, rather than it being a personal attack by you on them.
- If necessary, apply the sanction.
- If possible, allow the student to 'win' by offering a 'way out'.

Here's a brief example to show what I mean.

John arrives at the Drama studio and walks straight in, without taking off his shoes. The teacher has already set the rule that the students must take off their shoes before entering the room.

Teacher: John, please go back outside and take off your shoes.
    John: I can't, Miss.
Teacher: We have a rule in drama that we must take off our shoes.
    John: But I've sprained my ankle, Miss. I really can't take them off.
Teacher: Do you have a note about your ankle?
    John: No.
Teacher: Then please go back outside and take off your shoes.
    John: No. I won't.
Teacher: If you won't take off your shoes, then you will force me to give you a detention, John.
    John: That's not fair.
Teacher: Please go back outside and take off your shoes. Then I won't have to give you a detention.

At this point, John will either comply with the request, or the sanction must be applied. Just to show how differently this encounter might have turned out if the teacher didn't follow the guidelines, let's rerun the scene . . .

Teacher: John, go back outside and take off your shoes.

   John: I can't, Miss.

Teacher: What do you mean, 'I can't'. Of course you can.

   John: But I've sprained my ankle, Miss. I really can't take them off.

Teacher: Don't be so stupid.

   John: Don't call me stupid.

Teacher: Look, just go outside and take off your shoes. Now!

   John: No. I won't.

Teacher: Then you've got a detention with me after school.

   John: That's not fair. I'm not coming. Get stuffed!

Be calm and consistent

'I'm always fair and consistent with you.'

All of us welcome calmness and consistency. We like to know what to expect from other people, and when this consistency is missing and a difficult reaction occurs, we are both surprised and angered. It is not easy for teachers to remain calm and consistent on a daily basis. We are, of course, only human! If you are tired you may react badly to an incident of misbehaviour. However, if you can remain tirelessly calm, polite and consistent at all times, there will be far less possibility of serious confrontation, and you will also avoid creating unnecessary stress for yourself.

In interviews, the idea of 'fairness' came up frequently. Students felt that they, or their friends, were unfairly singled out, and once they had misbehaved, they were picked on over and over again. Similarly, there was a strong feeling that 'bad' teachers had their 'pets'. Perhaps we are all too often unaware of how our students actually perceive us. If we are honest, because we are human, we do in fact like some students more than others. The secret, of course, is not to let them know by showing our feelings in the way we behave.

When we were discussing sanctions, the students also mentioned that whole class punishments were extremely unfair, and of course they were right! Why on earth should they all be punished for the misbehaviour of a small minority? Let's take a look now at some of the times when you most need to be calm and consistent with your students:

- *The way your lessons run:* As we will see in the next chapter, it is essential that your lessons follow a pattern, and one that is as calm and consistent as possible. This pattern will allow your students to arrive at your classes knowing exactly what to expect from you, and knowing that you will remain cool whatever the circumstances. If their expectations are met on a regular basis, they will begin to feel a sense of security in your company, and will behave better as a result.

- *The way you interact with your students:* A calm, measured approach, and one that is similar every time they meet you, will help your students feel secure in your lessons. On the other hand, if they arrive at your class never knowing what sort of mood you are going to be in, they will be in a constant state of uncertainty about what to expect from you. However hard it might be, try to be in a good mood at all times!

- *The way you sanction your students:* The punishments that you give need to be applied calmly, to help reduce the tension that anyone feels when they are being disciplined. In addition to this, your sanctions must be seen to be fair and consistent. It is often tempting to punish a 'good' student less harshly than a 'bad' one, but this is something that teachers should avoid at all costs. The same infringement should nearly always result in the same reprimand. (As we will see later in the book, there are certain situations where you need to be flexible with your sanctions, for instance when dealing with a particularly difficult student.)

Give them structure

'I know where we're going.'
Our natural impulse is to place a structure on our lives – a daily pattern that gives us a feeling of safety and security. For many of the most difficult students in our schools, this structure is exactly what is missing from their world. At home, their parents or guardians may not have set boundaries for them, or they may constantly 'move the goalposts', reacting in a variety of different ways to the same types of misbehaviour. School can offer such young people a refuge, a place where they meet adults who give them suitable guidelines about what 'good' behaviour actually means.

How, then, do we as teachers offer our students 'structure'? What this means is, as a teacher, that you must have a very clear idea of where you are going with your class or classes. Your teaching must be structured, not only in terms of lesson content, but also in the way you organize your class and the way you control the behaviour of your students. Once you have a clear structure in your own mind, this clarity will be apparent to your class through your high level of awareness. In addition, you should make it blatantly clear to your students at every stage exactly how and why this structure is being used.

If you can achieve this strong sense of purpose, your students will know what to expect when they come to your class, and they will look forward to spending time with you. If their expectations are met every time they come into contact with you, they will start to view you as a stable feature of their lives, and their behaviour will become much more predictable and controllable. Let's look now at some aspects of your teaching that you can learn to structure:

- *The way your lessons will start and finish:* This aspect of your teaching is explored in some detail in the section entitled 'Be definite' earlier in this chapter. If the lesson starts and finishes in exactly the same way every time you see a class, they will soon learn to do these things automatically, making your life easier.
- *What will happen during the lesson:* Although the actual content of your lessons will vary according to what you are teaching that day, the way your lessons proceed will stay fairly constant. For instance, you might structure your lessons so that your classes are asked to work quietly, staying in their seats and putting up their hands if they do have any questions.
- *The aims and content of your lessons:* If your students are to be well motivated about their work, they must know what is going to happen during the lesson and why they need to learn these things. A simple way to achieve this is to state the aim of the lesson right at the start, and keep referring back to it throughout the class time. In this way, the students will have a very clear idea about what is going to happen during the lesson, giving them a sense of structure to hang on to. By explaining to them why the work is important, they will see a purpose and direction for the lesson you are doing.

- *Information about the work you want your students to achieve:* In addition to knowing about the content of the lesson, and the reasons why it is being taught, you should also give the students a very clear idea about exactly how much they need to achieve. One very useful way of doing this that was mentioned in the student interviews (see Chapter 9) is the teacher who says:
  - This is the work you *must* do.
  - This is the work you *should* do.
  - This is the work you *could* do.

  By dividing the work into these three categories, the students are given clear targets to aim at. The more able will probably finish all three parts of the work. The less able students know that there is a certain amount that must be completed if they are to avoid a sanction.
- *Details of what your students have actually achieved during the lesson:* It is always gratifying to look back on the time we have spent working on something and to feel a sense of achievement. If you are very clear with your students about what they have achieved, they will leave your lessons with a positive sense of success, and will be more likely to behave and work well the next time you see them.

Be positive

'You're doing great!'
Every teacher knows the mantra, 'stress the positive'. To be honest, it can sometimes feel as though we are praising our students for just about anything, to try to get them 'on our side'. I believe this is a mistake. If we set our sights low, then this low level is all our students will aim for. Whereas if we have high standards, and expect great things, our students will learn to strive for their best. Being positive is not just about praising your students, it is also about having a positive outlook during your time with them. The discriminating use of praise, and the ability to remain relentlessly positive, will help you a great deal with managing behaviour. In addition, it will probably make you a far less stressed out teacher!

Here are a few tips for staying positive with your students:

- frame everything you say in a positive light;

- try to avoid accusing your students or criticizing them;
- never use sarcasm – it really is 'the lowest form of wit', and can hurt children badly;
- react to misbehaviour by suggesting a positive alternative;
- use individual praise to encourage the whole class;
- constantly set targets to offer positive ways for your students to improve.

Let's look briefly at two examples of the same situation, a teacher inviting a class into the room, to show the difference between a positive and a negative approach.

Negative
'Come on, hurry up! Why are you being so slow? Come on, come on, we've got loads to get through today and we'll never get everything done if you're this slow. What's wrong with you? Why are you making so much noise?'

The problem here is the negative way the teacher is talking to the students. Immediately, they are criticized for being slow. The teacher then creates a negative feeling about the work they will be doing, by putting the blame on the students for not being able to get through it all. Finally, she uses two negative questions that both suggest the students are always this bad. By starting the lesson in such a negative frame of mind, the teacher's expectations may well be met!

Positive
'Right, if you can all come in as quickly as possible. I've got some really exciting things for you to do today, and we need to get started straight away, so that we can get through them all. That's an excellent level of noise. Well done. Now let's see if you can be even quieter.'

Here, instead of accusing the students of being 'slow', the teacher tells them how she wants them to come into the room. She then creates a sense of purpose and interest, by telling them that she has some 'really exciting' things planned for them. Finally, she praises them for the low level of noise, but sets them the challenge of being even quieter. By starting the lesson in this way, a positive atmosphere will be created and sustained.

2 Managing the first meeting

Why is the first meeting so important?

Your first meeting with any class offers you the chance to sow the seeds for an easy year, or to take the first step on the road to disaster. Every teacher must surely know that hollow feeling in the pit of the stomach, as you let a new class into your room for the very first time, aware that what you do in that very first meeting will have such a long-term impact. Often, both the teacher and the students will be feeling at their most defensive in the first lesson together. You may be anticipating bad behaviour from a 'difficult' class; they may be expecting you to dislike them if they know that other teachers feel negatively towards them.

With many classes, the first few meetings offer you a 'honeymoon period', where your students are getting to know you, 'checking you out' before revealing their true colours. If this is the type of class you have, make sure you don't start out with an overly relaxed attitude. If you do, you may find that a few lessons into the year, when the students have made a decision about your style as a teacher, they start to take advantage of your relaxed approach and begin to misbehave.

On the other hand, you may find yourself in a school where the students will misbehave for new teachers, testing them to see whether they can withstand the ordeal! This is obviously the more difficult situation to be in, and if you do find yourself at this type of school, you should very quickly turn to others to help and support you. Some ideas about how you might do this are given in Chapter 11.

What do you need to know before the first meeting?

Teachers are put in a very difficult position at the start of a school year (or at the start of the term, if they begin a new job midway through the year). They are expected to meet, control and teach a group of young people about whom they know little or nothing. Because of this, teachers have a tendency to learn by their mistakes, dealing with problems as they arise, rather than anticipating them.

Time is very precious at the start of term, and the other staff in your school are of course busy setting up their own classrooms, planning their first few lessons, emptying out their pigeonholes from the previous year, and so on. However, because of the vital importance of this first meeting with your new class or classes, it really is worth while taking some time to prepare. What exactly can you do in advance of meeting your classes? Here are some ideas for you to consider:

Knowledge is power

If possible, do try to find out some information about your students before you meet them for the first time. This will give you an advantage over your class – you know more about them than they do about you. It will also give you a psychological boost that could help you remain calm and confident. Here are some of the types of information that you might find useful:

- *Possible behaviour problems:* Is there a well-known trouble-maker in the class who you should watch out for? If you do know their name and also what is likely to 'set them off', you can keep an eye out for any early signs of misbehaviour. Sometimes a difficult student will be proud of their reputation. By acknowledging that their 'fame precedes them', you will show them that you are very aware as a teacher, a vital part of your basic armoury (see Chapter 1). In addition, you can offer them the chance of a 'fresh start', by pointing out that you will judge them solely by how they behave and work for you.
- *Learning needs:* Are there students with non-behavioural special needs that may have an impact on their learning? Such special needs can be perceived incorrectly by a teacher, and wrongly interpreted as a behavioural difficulty. For instance, if a student has great difficulty in writing, they may not complete the work set. If you misinterpret this as

laziness, you will fail to meet their needs, and you could also provoke misbehaviour.

- *Physical needs:* If there a student with a hearing problem or other physical difficulty that you should take into consideration? Although such an impediment may not necessarily be a recipe for misbehaviour, there are certain things that you should do as a teacher to avoid embarrassing such a student. For instance, a student with a hearing problem may not follow an instruction, because they have not heard you, and you might misinterpret this as rudeness. In addition, you will be aware that you should avoid shouting at this particular student.

- *Knowing the names:* It can also be very useful to know the names of one or two of your students, as the class will be amazed and impressed if you can use a name correctly, apparently without ever having been told it. Knowing your students' names really is vital in controlling the class (see 'Learn some names' in this chapter).

In your pursuit of knowledge, do remember that it is vitally important to avoid prejudging your classes. Not only is this likely to put you in a negative frame of mind; it is also unfair on the students. Some students who have a bad reputation in a school are never given a chance to prove this reputation is false. Give them the chance to impress you and you may be pleasantly surprised!

Your teaching style

Before you meet a class for the first time, you should have made a definite decision about the style of teaching you will offer them. Are you going to be a 'firm but fun' teacher whose lessons are varied, interesting and enjoyable? Or are you going to be a 'strict and scary' teacher who wants them to push themselves to the maximum every time? (See Chapter 9 – 'What the students said' – for more information on these two types of teachers.)

Of course, teachers develop their own individual style through experience, but it may be that you sometimes need to change or modify your particular style to suit a specific class. Teachers who are good managers of behaviour adapt their style to fit their students, depending on their age, personalities and so on. You can find more information about adapting your behaviour to fit your students in Chapter 11 ('Age-specific strategies').

There are many different aspects of your 'style' that will affect the way your students perceive you. These are explored in detail in Chapter 4, but here are a few ideas about some areas of your style that will be under immediate examination:

- *The way you appear:* Are you smart, wearing a suit, or do you dress casually? Do you seem ready to meet and teach the class, or are you flustered and bad tempered when they arrive? Interviewers make their minds up about a candidate in the first few minutes of an interview, based mainly on how they look. If you want your classes to behave, you need to make a good impression on them the first time you meet them too!

- *The way you treat your students:* Do you regard your students as equals, or do you see yourself as 'better' than them? Do you respect them and talk to them politely, whatever the provocation? Remember, when you are working with and disciplining individual students, particularly early on, your whole class will be watching and observing you, making a decision about how they are going to behave for you in the future.

- *The way you start and finish your lessons:* Do the students arrive at your first lesson, and find that it begins and ends in a calm, controlled way? Or do you run out of time and rush them out of the room? Do you put them in a good mood from the first minute they meet you? And do they leave you feeling that they have had a positive experience, one that they want to repeat? Never is this more important than the very first time you meet a class.

- *The way you teach your lessons:* Is the lesson varied, interesting, challenging and fun? I know very well that this is a tall order, but you should certainly try very hard to make your first experience with a class a positive one in terms of the lesson content. If you can captivate your students early on, they are far more likely to come to your class in a constructive frame of mind, ready and eager to learn.

- *The way you control the class:* Are you a 'strict and scary' teacher, who shouts at the class from the very first moment you meet them? Are you 'firm but fair', controlling them through the subtle strength of your personality? Or do you greet them timidly, immediately allowing them to feel they are in charge and not you? Your students will be examining the way you keep control from the very first meeting.

What do you need to do in the first meeting?

Set up the pattern of your lessons

The first lesson is a stressful experience for both teacher and students. There can be very few people who really enjoy a totally new encounter, where they know little or nothing about what is going to happen, and what the people involved are going to be like. So, as ever, you need to give your classes structure, by running your lessons in a controlled and consistent way. There are many different ways that you can give your lessons a structure or pattern, and probably the best way to illustrate this is to give an example.

So here is an account of one way of doing things. This lesson lasts one hour and the exact timing is given. In addition, I have made some comments about reasons why this particular pattern is used. As you will notice, it is first thing in the morning. Mr Charman, the class's new maths teacher, is at his freshest, ready for this first meeting! The class is fairly amenable. (See Chapter 3, 'Control techniques', for some ideas about what to do if it is not!) This example is not necessarily ideal. It is just one illustration of a possible lesson pattern:

9.00: The bell goes. Mr Charman checks that he has everything ready, then goes to wait outside the room, closing the door behind him.

> **Comment:** The teacher starts the lesson by indicating his status, almost 'marking his territory'. By standing outside the room, with the door closed, he creates a physical and mental barrier between the students and his space. He is well prepared for the actual teaching, he 'knows where they're going' (see Chapter 1).

9.03: The students arrive at the classroom in dribs and drabs. Mr Charman is standing waiting for them at the door, arms folded. He is clearly ready for them, and looks imposing. Quietly, he asks the students to line up, in single file, until everyone arrives.

> **Comment:** The pattern for every lesson is being set. The class will line up outside the room until they have all arrived, a useful way of imposing order (see 'Be definite' in Chapter 1). As yet, Mr Charman has not addressed the class as a whole. He is waiting to do this until the majority arrive.

9.07: Mr Charman looks very deliberately at his watch. He is now ready to begin. He gets the students silent, then talks to them briefly about what they should do once inside the room.

> **Comment:** The teacher has been quite lenient with the time here, as he does not want to set up confrontations at the start of his first lesson. However, he will explain his exact requirements for the future once the class are inside the room.

9.10: The class are settled in their seats, and Mr Charman begins by explaining how his lessons will run. He sets some boundaries (see Chapter 3) and makes it clear why these are necessary.

> **Comment:** Although the teacher will normally go straight into teaching the content of his lessons, he has a little leeway during this first meeting, when the class are willing to listen to him, to find out what he has to say. He uses this opportunity to make his boundaries very clear, whilst his students are at their most receptive.

9.15: Now Mr Charman begins the lesson proper. He takes out a £5 note and asks the class what it is. When they tell him that it is worth five pounds, and could he please give it to them, he expresses surprise. '*But it's just a piece of paper, isn't it!*' he says, and starts to tear it into tiny pieces.

> **Comment:** The teacher will certainly have got the class's attention by doing this. (And don't worry, the £5 note is, of course, a fake.) The students should now be engaged and keen to find out what the lesson is going to be about. They will probably also discuss the lesson with other students after it is over, a very useful way of earning yourself a reputation (see the section in Chapter 4, 'Create a reputation').

9.20: Mr Charman now explains the aim of this particular lesson, which is an exploration of the role of money in society, different currencies, and so on. The class are set a discussion task, which will take them ten minutes.

9.30: The class finish the discussion task and share what they have brainstormed.

9.40: Mr Charman sets a brief written task, which will be completed for homework.

> **Comment:** The pattern of this teacher's lessons is being set. He will start every lesson by explaining the work he aims to do. His classes will include a lot of variety and keep the students' interest throughout. Today, he uses an introduction (teacher addressing class); a period for the students to brainstorm what they already know (group discussion); a session for the class to share what they have discussed (teacher leading with the students listening to each other); and then a written task to reinforce the learning (individual written work), with homework to complete.

9.53: Because this is the first lesson, the teacher leaves plenty of time for clearing up. He stops the class, gets silence, and then explains the pattern for the end of every lesson. The students will write their homework down and then clear away their books.

9.57: The students have now put their stuff away, and the teacher gets silence, then asks them to stand behind their chairs.

> **Comment:** By ending early, Mr Charman has time to praise his students for their hard work, setting up a 'good feeling' about the time they have spent together. He can also make clear his expectations about the completion of homework, or answer any last minute queries.

Learn some names

When you are endeavouring to control student behaviour, you are at a great disadvantage if you do not know the names of the people in your classes. All too often, I have seen (and experienced) students taking advantage of a teacher who does not know their names. This must surely be the worst part of working as a supply teacher – it is all too easy for students to give you the wrong name without you knowing. And if you do not have their correct names, you have little chance of imposing sanctions, such as detentions, or reporting badly behaved students to a higher authority. There are various methods you can use to learn your students' names as quickly as possible. Here are some suggestions for you to consider when preparing for your first meeting:

- *Use a seating plan:* Not only is a seating plan a good way of learning names, but it is also an excellent method of demonstrating control over the class. In the interviews, this was a feature that came up several times when the students were describing 'a teacher who is good at keeping control'.
- *Use memory systems:* If you don't yet know about memory systems, there are some excellent books on the market to help you learn. These systems really can be a very useful asset for teachers, particularly when learning names. The basic idea is the use of 'hooks', or connections between things. For instance, you might have a student called

David who looks a little like a well-known footballer, or you could teach a child named Ben, who is very big (think 'Big Ben'!).

- *Make notes on your register:* A few subtle, well-placed annotations on your register will help you a great deal when learning students' names. When you mark the register, look to see which student answers and, if they have a particular distinguishing characteristic (such as wearing glasses), make a brief note of this to help you remember. Do, however, avoid writing anything embarrassing or rude, in case someone else takes a look at your register!
- *Set yourself a target:* Faced with a sea of children, the task of learning all those names can seem huge, especially if you are a secondary school teacher, perhaps teaching hundreds of different students. You could set yourself a reasonable target, aiming to learn three to five names per lesson, with the aim that within a few weeks you will have learnt the names of all the students in each class.

When you are teaching a badly behaved class, it is all too easy to focus on the troublemakers and to learn their names first. You may find, as a result, that you never get to learn the names of the 'nice' or quiet students in your class. This is a shame, although it is a mistake that many teachers (including me) do make. Do try, then, to focus on at least one or two quiet students in your first meeting, getting to know them too.

Set the boundaries
There is more information in the next chapter about how you can set boundaries with your classes, and the first meeting is an ideal time to do this, when your students are likely to be reasonably receptive. If you set your boundaries now, and stick to them consistently every time you meet the class, the students will quickly learn to follow them automatically.

Demonstrate your 'teaching style'
As explained earlier in this chapter, you need to give a clear indication of your style as a teacher. Style is a rather nebulous concept, but it is crucial to your success as a manager of behaviour.

Chapter 4 deals with this concept in some detail. Don't forget, you are 'flying solo', with 30 or so pairs of eyes focused on you alone. Like an actor on press night, you should give the performance of your life in that first meeting!

Reducing the stress of the first meeting

Remember that for your students, too, this is the first time they have met you. As yet, they have formed little or no opinion of you. If you are an 'old hand' at your school, your reputation will precede you, particularly if there are brothers and sisters of students you have already taught in the class. But if you are a new teacher at the school, you are currently the 'mystery man or woman', an unknown entity, and consequently of great interest to your students.

If the class do misbehave, it is very easy for your confidence to drop, especially in your first lesson. Here are a few tips for reducing the stress if this does happen:

- *Stay calm and relaxed:* If the students see you becoming tense and angry, you are giving them an incentive to misbehave in future. An explosive reaction might be just what they want to get from you! However hard it is (and I know it's hard) you must stay calm. Breathe deeply, pull yourself together, and deal with it.
- *React from the head:* As you feel yourself tensing up, and reacting emotionally rather than intellectually, make a conscious decision not to let your heart win the day. There is a more detailed explanation of this technique in Chapter 3.
- *Don't become defensive:* Remind yourself constantly that this is *not* personal. If your students 'attack' your lesson by misbehaving, do not respond by defending yourself and becoming overly hostile. A far more useful and assertive way to respond is to attack back by being relentlessly positive.
- *Follow the 'basic rules':* Particularly the first three – be definite, be aware, and be calm and consistent.

And if all else fails . . .

- *Don't be a perfectionist:* Let's face it, it is not a total disaster if a few students muck around in your first lesson. The world is not going to end. You are not going to get the sack. And you will have plenty of time to win them back.

3 Control techniques

How do I gain and keep control?

Controlling a large group of people is difficult in any situation, but when some of your students have no wish to be in school, let alone in your lesson, life can become very difficult indeed. In addition to using the basic techniques in Chapter 1, there are various other ways that you can create and maintain an ordered yet relaxed atmosphere in your classroom. These techniques are easy to apply, and should cost you little in the way of stress. The majority of the tips given below are connected to the idea of remaining calm. And if you can achieve a serene atmosphere in your lessons, you are far more likely to receive good behaviour in return from your students.

- Wait for silence
- Always be polite
- Avoid confrontation
- React from the head
- Use the deadly stare
- Control your voice
- Use repetition
- Personalize your teaching
- Know when to be flexible
- Set the boundaries
- Set them targets
- Intervene early
- Remove the problem

Wait for silence

Waiting for silence is one of the most important, useful and easily achievable control techniques that any teacher can use. When I say 'wait for silence', what I mean is that you should not address your students until they are *completely* silent and fully focused on you. This applies not only at the start of the lesson, for instance when taking the register, but also at any time when you wish to address your students. There are several ways of getting silence from your class:

- *The force of your personality:* If you are teaching a well-behaved and attentive group of students, you may well find that simply standing with your arms folded and looking mean will achieve the required result. Some teachers do manage to control very difficult students solely by using the strength of their personality, but it takes time, experience, and an extremely strong character to do this.
- *The well-chosen phrase:* If your class are more difficult, you may need to tell them to be quiet, then wait until you have achieved total silence before continuing. If necessary, repeat the phrase several times over, pausing briefly to gauge the students' response. Try using some of the following phrases to gain silence:
    - *'I'd like you all to look this way and listen very carefully.'*
    - *'Looking at me and listening please.'*
    - *'I'm going to wait for complete silence until I continue.'*
    - *'I want silence in five ... four ... three ... two ... one!'*
    (See 'Set them targets' below.)
- *The non-verbal 'silence command':* In some subjects or situations, you may need to use a recognized signal to achieve silence. For instance, in PE or Drama, or in a class of very young children, the students may be engaged in a noisy activity that would require you to shout to be heard. If you can avoid shouting, you will not only save your voice, but you will also maintain that wonderful calm atmosphere you have worked so hard to achieve. You will need to train your class to respond quickly to your signal, practising and praising them until they react in the correct way. Here are some examples of 'silence commands':
    - The use of a whistle.
    - 'Hands up' – the teacher raises their hand for silence and the class must stop what they are doing, put their hands up, and be quiet.

– The 'silent seat' – the teacher sits down in a designated seat, and the children must come to sit in front of her (or in their chairs) and be silent.

In your first lesson with a class, you should talk to them about why you have set this particular boundary, one that they *must* learn to follow. In addition to listening to you in silence, your goal should always be that they learn to listen to each other quietly as well. There are several reasons why they need to learn to do this, and you could discuss these ideas with them and also ask them for any other reasons they can think of. By sharing the discussion with your class, your students will understand the purpose behind your demand more fully. Here are some ideas about why they should be silent:

- so that they can hear instructions;
- so that they can learn effectively;
- to show respect for the teacher;
- to show respect for each other;
- because they would want others to listen silently to them;
- for their own safety (in case you need to give them an urgent command);
- because it's polite!

To strengthen this instruction, you could point out to your class that you don't speak while others are talking, that you always listen to what they have to say, and they must reciprocate in kind.

Always be polite

When faced with students who are rude to you, it is all too easy to react in kind. However, if you can achieve it, a relentlessly polite manner will help you to defuse the most difficult situations. In addition, you will be setting the most appropriate example of good behaviour that you can. When disciplining recalcitrant students, always remember the rest of your class are watching and learning from you. If they see you remaining calm and polite whatever the provocation, they will see that you are in the right and the student who misbehaves is in the wrong.

Let's look now at an example of misbehaviour, and how the teacher might react in two very different ways. In this example, Jackie is refusing to complete the work that the teacher has set. In the first instance, notice how the comments very quickly become a 'tit-for-tat' battle of rudeness, a confrontation that the rest of the class will be observing with interest. In the second situation, you can see the teacher defusing every rude comment that Jackie makes, leaving her with nowhere to go. You will find more information on this technique for deflecting insults in Chapter 4.

Reacting 'in kind'
Teacher: Jackie, get on with your work and stop causing problems.
  Jackie: No I won't. This work is stupid and your lessons are boring!
Teacher: No, Jackie, you're stupid and boring, not the work.
  Jackie: Don't you call me stupid and boring, you old cow.
Teacher: How dare you call me an old cow! Right, you're in detention.
  Jackie: Oh yeah? Well I'm not staying behind with *you*. I hate you.
Teacher: And I hate you too. *[Shouting]* NOW GET ON WITH THE WORK!

Being relentlessly polite
Teacher: Jackie, please could you get on with your work now.
  Jackie: No I won't. This work is stupid and your lessons are boring!
Teacher: I'm very sorry that you feel like that. Now please do the work.
  Jackie: No I won't! You're an old cow!
Teacher: Well, I might be a *cow*, but I'm not *that* old, am I Jackie?
  Jackie: *[totally confused by this response]* What?
Teacher: Now please could you get on with the work. You have ten minutes to finish and I'd love to see how well you can do.

Avoid confrontation

Whenever possible, teachers should always avoid getting into a confrontation with their students. Not only will this lessen the chance of a negative encounter spiralling out of control; it will also dissipate any tension and give you a far less stressful life. Students become confrontational for a variety of different reasons. It could be that they have learnt from example, from parents or guardians who react to problems in a confrontational manner. The student might feel embarrassed to have their poor behaviour challenged and react in an aggressive way to hide their discomfort.

How, then, do we avoid becoming confrontational with our students? After all, when you're tired and stressed, and a student swears at you or behaves in a completely inappropriate way, it is all too easy to confront the behaviour in a similarly hostile way, thus escalating the situation. Avoiding confrontation does not mean you don't deal with the issue, though. It means you approach the problem in a sensitive manner. When you take on a confrontational student, try to use some of the following techniques:

- *Remain calm:* I make no apologies for repeating this idea again, because I know how important it is. Think about it – have you ever tried arguing with someone who will not argue back? It's very difficult to sustain feelings of anger when you have nothing to feed off. If you can remain calm at all times, it will be that much harder for your students to sustain a confrontational manner.
- *Change the subject:* If a confrontation does arise, it can sometimes be dissipated by this technique. Just as, when a baby is crying, you might try pulling a silly face or shaking a favourite toy, so by changing the subject with your students, you could throw them 'off the track' of their aggression.
- *Allow them to 'win':* This is tough. You're human. You're in the right. Why on earth should you allow the student to 'win'? There are three reasons for using this strategy. First, some confrontational students could become completely out of control, and you may have no hope of winning them back or distracting them. Second, you will end the confrontation and save yourself undue stress. And last, remember that you only need to make the student *feel* that they have won. In your own head, you know that you are really in the right.

React from the head

It is very easy, when faced with a rude and aggressive student, to react emotionally, taking the treatment to heart. In fact, this is the natural thing to do: you're a human being and not a machine, after all! But what you have to remember is, if you do become emotional, not only will you be stressing yourself – you will also be allowing the student to win the challenge. What many difficult students want is to do is 'wind up' the teacher, and if you allow yourself to react emotionally, they will have succeeded.

If at all possible, every time you feel your heart starting to race, and an emotional reaction kicking in, take a moment to think about the situation from your head rather than from your heart. What this means is, to respond in an intellectual, thinking way, rather than in a sensitive, feeling way. Let's take a look at a couple of examples, to illustrate this point more fully. The teacher's possible emotional and intellectual reactions to each situation are shown.

The disruptive student

Matthew is wandering around the room, disturbing the rest of the class and refusing to sit back down, despite being warned about possible sanctions.

Your heart says: *'Why won't he do what I say? The rest of the class must think I've got no control over him. I feel so helpless. Now I'm getting angry. WHY WON'T YOU DO WHAT I SAY, MATTHEW?'*

Your head says: *'Okay, this student is refusing to do what I say, but it's not my fault, it's his own choice. Now, what am I going to do about it? Well, first of all I'll stay calm, that's important. Then I'll warn him, and if that doesn't work, impose the sanctions I've told the class about.'*

The uncontrollable class

Your class is an extremely difficult one, and they are totally refusing to settle down and get on with their work. They are making loads of noise and throwing paper aeroplanes around the room.

Your heart says: *'Help!!! They're completely out of control! What am I going to do!? Someone might hear them and think I can't control my classes. I'm never ever going to be able to get them settled down and teach them! Why did I ever decide to become a teacher?'*

Your head says: *'Okay, things are going wrong here, but I'm not* *going to panic. First of all, it's not my fault, it's the students who have decided to misbehave. And everyone says what a difficult class this is. I'll try and apply the sanctions I've set, and if necessary I'll have to keep the whole class in. I know, I'll write "whole class detention?" on the board and see if that helps.'*

Use the deadly stare

We all know examples of teachers who can simply walk in a room and the class will fall silent, teachers who can control their classes perfectly, but who never have to raise their voices. Although there are many factors that come together to create this lucky type of teacher, perhaps one of the most important is that of non-verbal communication. In teaching, your face is one of your most important tools, and the use of the 'deadly stare' can be extremely effective.

The deadly stare is part of what the students are talking about when they say a teacher looks like they know what they want. If you can perfect the deadly stare, you will save yourself a great deal of time spent in giving verbal commands. To illustrate this, I'd like to use the analogy of the teacher being like an actor. Behind the deadly stare is the knowledge (or at least the pretence) that you 'know what you want' and you 'know what will happen if you don't get what you want' (see Chapter 1). If you can achieve this mental attitude, or at least give the impression you feel this way, your face will communicate your deadly state of mind.

The deadly stare is difficult to describe, but you will certainly know when you have mastered it. The deadly stare tells your students they must do what you want, or they are likely to suffer the ghastly consequences, something that is clearly *not* recommended! And all this without even having to talk to them!

Control your voice

Just as with your face, your voice is a tool, an instrument that you must use every single day of your working life. When we are in a stressful situation, our voices can very easily betray our emotions, becoming louder, or cracking under pressure. When faced with poor behaviour, your voice will give your students a very clear indication of your emotional state, and they will respond to the signals they are given by the way you talk.

As we have already seen, the ideal is for the students to see you reacting from your head and not from your heart. The secret is for you to be in control of the way you sound at all times. If you need to change the volume or tone of your voice, this should be a conscious decision rather than as a result of emotional stress. Here are some ideas about how you can use your voice effectively:

- *Control the volume when teaching:* The quieter you are as a teacher, the quieter your classes will have to be to hear you. In my first book, *Starting Teaching*, I pointed out that 'quiet teachers get quiet classes', and I have always found this to be true. When bringing down the volume level in your lessons, simply use the image of turning down the sound on a stereo. Ask yourself: how loud do I need to be for my students to hear me? In this way, you will ensure your students are attentive – they will need to be to hear you!

- *Control the volume when disciplining students:* In addition to controlling the volume during your teaching, if you can discipline students in a quiet way you should find that their behaviour improves as a result. When you are talking to an individual student about their behaviour, get close to them and talk so that only they can hear. An additional benefit of this technique is that you will prevent the rest of the class being an 'audience' to your comments.

- *Control the tone:* In addition to perfecting the deadly stare, you should be able to put a deadly tone into your voice that tells your students when you are *not* happy. If you can manage to change your tone of voice at a moment's notice, you will make it perfectly clear what your 'feelings' are (not necessarily your actual emotions, but what you choose to put across as such).

Use repetition

Repetition is a vitally important tool when controlling behaviour. Much of the time, when we say something in the classroom, we expect it to be heard and understood the first time around. This is not necessarily a sensible expectation to have, and it may lead to unnecessary confrontations. Classrooms are often noisy and confusing places for our students, and there could be many different reasons why they do not respond immediately to your directions. Here are some good reasons why teachers should use repetition:

- To get a student's attention before you give them an instruction, or warn them about a sanction.
- Because your students might not hear your instructions the first time you give them.
- To clarify any possible misunderstandings and make your wishes perfectly clear.
- In order to reinforce your instructions and make it clear that they must be followed.

There are various things you might need to repeat when sanctioning a student:

- The name of the student, to get their attention.
- The instruction you have given. (You could also ask the student to repeat this, to check that they have understood.)
- The options for avoiding a sanction.
- The sanction you are imposing, if they fail to comply.

Let's look specifically at how you could use repetition during an incident of misbehaviour. In this example, Adrian is chatting to his friends rather than doing his work:

Teacher: Adrian.

The teacher waits, there is no response.

Teacher: Adrian. I'd like you to look at me and listen.
 Adrian: What, miss?

He is still looking at his friends.

Teacher: Adrian. I said I'd like you to look at me and listen, please.

Finally, he turns around and looks at the teacher.

Teacher: Thank you, Adrian. Right, I want you to get on with your
         work right now. No more talking please.
 Adrian: Okay then.

He turns back, but continues chatting.

Teacher: Oh Adrian?

Adrian: Yeah?

Teacher: Could you repeat what I just said? What was my instruction?

Adrian: To get on with my work and stop talking.

Teacher: Good. I'm glad you understand. I'd hate to have to give you a detention, but I will if you don't stop chatting and get on with your work.

Personalize your teaching

In the interviews, many of the students commented that they wanted their teachers to 'get to know them'. They had a strong preference for teachers who treated them as individuals, and who got to know their personal strengths and weaknesses, likes and dislikes, and so on. They commented that they were far more likely to behave well for a teacher who could achieve this 'personal' factor in their classes. No one likes to be told off, but just imagine your reaction if a complete stranger walked up to you in the street and reprimanded you for something you had done. When we first meet our students, we know very little about them, and until they can see that we are going to treat them as real people, their reaction is likely to be negative when we do have to discipline them.

In the primary and middle school, where teachers work mainly with just one class, they can get to know their students as individuals fairly quickly, and can then take steps to personalize their teaching. In the secondary school, where a teacher may face many different classes in the course of a week, it is naturally harder to do this, but it is still just as important. How, then, can you personalize your teaching? Here are some ideas that might help you.

- *Personalize the work:* Try to find out what interests your students, and incorporate this into your work. For instance, at any given time, children will be in the grips of the latest 'craze', be it Pokémon, Tamagotchi, Gameboys, Manchester United, the Spice Girls, or whatever else the most recent fashion is. If you can, at times, relate the work that you do to these trends (or other things that interest your students), they will feel far more personally engaged. Chapter 6 gives more ideas about how you might do this.

- *Personalize your discipline methods:* When you are disciplining individual students, you should try and mould your methods to the person. What I mean by this is, some students will react well to a strict, scary approach, whilst others will respond only to a quiet, firm hand. As you get to know your students, you will quickly learn about their personal 'discipline requirements'.

- *Talk to them!:* Try to spend a little time in each lesson talking to your students on an individual basis. Make them feel that you want to get to know the 'real' them, and you are likely to get better behaviour in return. In addition, if you can include your students in much of the decision-making that goes on in class, for instance when setting the rules, they will feel a sense of personal involvement in your lessons and the boundaries that you set.

- *Get to know them outside lesson time:* If you can become involved in some form of extra curricular activity, for instance running a football club, or helping out with the school play, your students will learn to see you as a person, rather than just as a teacher. Another excellent idea is to organize a trip for them, one of the most positive and memorable experiences many students will have during their school career.

Know when to be flexible

There are times as a teacher when you need to learn how to bend a little, for your students' sake and also for your own. Sometimes, and only sometimes, you will need to relax your boundaries, accept that you are not going to achieve everything that you want, and show your students that you are capable of being human. This flexibility is very much a matter of personal taste, and will depend a great deal on how much of a perfectionist you are. Here are a few ideas about how and when you could offer your students flexibility:

- *With the class:* If you teach a difficult class last thing on a Friday afternoon, and they are never in the mood for work, then you will achieve very little if you cannot learn to be flexible. Accept, in your mind, that this situation is outside your control, and aim to achieve a very reasonable amount of work with them, talking to them about how fair you are being. The same situation might apply if you have to teach a class last thing in the day, directly after their PE lesson. If your students turn up still in their PE kit, it is up to you whether you feel you want to allow them this small compromise in terms of uniform.

- *With the work:* On occasions, when your class is not 'in the mood' for whatever reason, you might like to offer your students a compromise. If they can complete a part of the work that you specify, then you could allow them to chat quietly for a few minutes at the end of the lesson as a reward.

- *With the individual:* Some students simply do not want to be in school (see Chapter 7, 'Why do students misbehave?', for some more thoughts on this problem). If you find yourself in a situation where an individual student just will not work for you, do try to see whether you can be flexible about how you treat them. Ask yourself how much stress it is worth for you to discipline them to work. How much will they actually achieve if you do confront them repeatedly? And how much damage will you do to your relationship if you do take this approach?

Set the boundaries

Although discussion of this technique has come towards the end of the chapter, it is possibly one of the most important ways of controlling behaviour in your classes. Setting boundaries for your students means giving them limits, a set of invisible barriers beyond which they must not go. As I have already said, everyone wants structure in their lives, and no one more so than your most badly behaved students. You have the responsibility, as their teacher, for training them to stay within acceptable boundaries.

Setting clear boundaries will mean that your students see you as a 'definite' and 'aware' teacher, one that they cannot 'get one over' on. The boundaries that you set will be to do with all aspects of your classroom practice. You will need to set boundaries for the work –

how much work needs to be done, and how well must it be completed? You will also need to set boundaries for behaviour – how should your students behave towards you and towards each other? Once you have set your boundaries, and talked them through with your students, you must stick to them on a consistent basis. And if your students do choose to push at the barriers you have given them, you must be prepared to sanction them accordingly.

Let's take a look at some of the issues you need to consider when setting your boundaries:

Boundaries for learning
- How will the students know what the lesson is about?
- How should they treat their learning, and that of others?
- How will the learning be reinforced?
- What is the reward for hard work and a positive learning experience?
- What is the sanction for lack of hard work?
- How and when is homework set?
- What happens if homework is not completed?

Boundaries for behaviour
- How should the students behave towards you?
- How should they behave towards each other?
- What types of behaviour are unacceptable?
- What will happen if the students do behave in an unacceptable way?
- What types of behaviour are desired and acceptable?
- What is the reward for students who do behave 'correctly'?

Set them targets

In my experience, children can be surprisingly competitive, and the sensible teacher will capitalize on this competitive streak in their students. The idea is not to set them at each other's throats, but to give them a clear objective to aim for, and a good reason to strive to reach it. As I have mentioned before, we all like structure in our lives, and a target gives us something definite to work towards. By setting targets, both for work and for behaviour, we can encourage our students to reach for their best. We might set a target for the amount of time a piece of work takes to complete, or a target for how well the work should be done. We could set a target for improving our students' behaviour, such as staying in their seats, or putting up their hands when they want to ask a question. To illustrate this idea further, here are some examples of a teacher setting targets for his/her class:

A whole class target for work

'Right. Today we're going to have a competition. As you can see, I've written ten questions up on the board about the work we did last lesson. The first person to answer all ten, in full sentences, can be teacher for ten minutes. Ready, steady, go!' (See Chapter 5 – 'Types of rewards' – for an explanation of this prize.)

An individual target for work

'Okay, Arwel. What I want you to do today is to concentrate on putting full stops in your writing, but they must be in the right place. Don't worry too much about spelling, because today we're going to focus on the punctuation. And if you do manage to put all the full stops in, you can choose one of these fantastic stickers.'

A whole class target for behaviour

'Right, class, looking this way and listening very carefully please. That's superb. Today we're going to have a test. [Groans from the class.] No! Not that kind of test. This is a test to see who has the best self-discipline in the class. And there's a very special prize for the winner. I want to see who can work in silence for the longest time, and the best person gets to eat this chocolate bar in front of the whole class!'

An individual target for behaviour

'Now then, Chris, I know how hard you find it to stay in your seat, so today I'm going to set you a challenge. If you can stay in your chair for the whole lesson, without getting up once, you can win three whole merits. I'll give you one merit for every twenty minutes that you manage to sit still. Okay?'

Intervene early

When an incident of misbehaviour starts, early intervention can help prevent the situation from building up, and from turning into a full-blown confrontation. Teachers need to be 'on their toes' at all times, keeping an eye out for the early signs of a problem. When you do notice an argument starting, or a student becoming restless, if you can intercede straight away you may well be able to stop the trouble before it really starts. In Chapter 13, you can see some examples of what might happen if a teacher does or doesn't follow this advice.

In addition to intervening early with a small-scale problem, the same idea applies with your classes. If you do notice that a particular group is becoming very chatty, or is starting to challenge your authority, make sure that you clamp down on the situation right away. Reinforce your power, perhaps by using a seating plan for several lessons, or by getting the students to line up outside the room rather than allowing them inside as they arrive. You can see an example of a teacher using this technique in Chapter 12.

Remove the problem

In addition to intervening early, another good way of avoiding conflicts is to remove the issue from the equation. It could be that you remove a child from the classroom for a while, to calm them down and stop an argument developing. Or it could be that you take an item from a student, if it is distracting them from their work, or if they are quarrelling about its rightful ownership and consequently disrupting your lesson.

Confrontations can often start because of the things that your students bring into the classroom from outside. On countless occasions, I have seen students get into an argument over a pencil case, a set of felt tips, a Pokémon card, a CD, or a mobile phone. *'It's mine!'* one will say. *'No it's not, it's mine!'* the other will respond. These sort of situations are difficult for a teacher to deal with, because many students are extremely possessive (and rightly so) over their belongings. The ideal is for the teacher to remove the problem, by confiscating the item from the student concerned. That way, the lesson is not disrupted, and the issue can be settled outside of class time. In reality, this can be hard to do, because you must make the student give you the article, rather than physically removing it from them.

If the thing causing the conflict is actually banned from school, you have every right to take it, passing it on to the head teacher, or the relevant senior person. On the other hand, if your taking the item away is going to cause increased friction, it might be better to simply demand that the student puts it back in their bag, and to warn them that if you do see it again, they will have to hand it over to you. Again, you will see some examples of a teacher dealing with this type of problem in Chapter 12.

Part Two

The Teacher and the Teaching

4 Teaching styles

What is a teaching style?

There are of course as many styles of teaching as there are teachers, because we are all individuals who work in our own unique ways. On the other hand, there are certain aspects of our individual style that we can make conscious decisions about, in order to help us conrol our students' behaviour. There are many different things that go together to make up a teaching style: the way you look, the way you speak, the way you keep control, in fact everything you do will add to your students' perception of your style. And an effective teaching style will show your class that *you* are in charge. But how exactly do you achieve 'an effective teaching style'?

Showing who's in charge

Your students want a teacher who they feel is in charge. They said so in the interviews! That way, they can feel secure within the boundaries that you set, safe in the knowledge that what you say goes. Showing that you are in charge can seem like a rather indefinable, nebulous idea. You might feel that other teachers seem to have a natural ability to appear in control, while you flounder in the dark, unsure of how exactly it is done. Well, we're going to see in this section that there are some easy, practical ways to show that you, too, are in charge!

What you want to achieve is a high level of status in the classroom: for your students to look up to you, respect you, and consequently behave for you. However, at the same time you should preserve the impression that you are human too, and also that you view each and every one of your students as an important individual. It should be possible for you to be in charge without being seen as overbearing. How, then, can you do this?

Physical aspects

The teacher is a very physical presence in the classroom, and much of what you communicate to your students is done in a physical way, whether consciously or unconsciously. Looking at your physical 'personality' is, after all, one of the main ways that your students perceive you, and you should therefore think carefully about the physical aspects of your teaching persona, particularly if you are not naturally good at appearing 'in charge'. A great deal of the skill of appearing 'definite' and 'aware' (see Chapter 1) comes from the way that you use your body. Here are some ideas for you to consider:

- *Use your face:* This is what your students spend the majority of their time looking at. If they see your face constantly moving, smiling and relaxed, but always alert, then they will believe that you are in charge.
- *Use your eyes:* When you're addressing the class, keep your eyes moving around, checking that all the faces are staring right back at you. If they're not, wait. Remember: never, ever talk until you have *everyone's* attention. By using your eyes to scan around the classroom during your lessons, you might catch an incident of misbehaviour before it starts, and be able to 'nip it in the bud'.
- *Use your voice:* As we saw in Chapter 3, your voice is an indicator for your students of how definite and aware you feel in the classroom. Teachers spend a great deal of time talking, and your voice is a crucial aspect of your individual style. Are you a loud teacher, who likes to shout, or a quiet teacher, who prefers the deadly stare? Whichever style you choose, make sure that you keep your voice relaxed and under control at all times.
- *Use your body:* Our bodies can inadvertently reveal our innermost feelings, and if we want to be seen as in control, we must be conscious of what our body language is saying. Try to avoid becoming closed in and defensive with your body, particularly during an incident of misbehaviour. If

you can keep your body relaxed and open, your students will respond so much better to you.

- *Dress for success:* Whether you choose to dress smartly or casually, your students will be making decisions about your style from looking at your clothes. A smart appearance does tend to make a good impression, although teachers of certain subjects will be restricted in what they can wear, because of the requirements of their curriculum area.

Spatial aspects

The way that you use the space in which you teach will communicate a complex message about your style, and about whether you are in control. When we are feeling defensive, it is tempting to back into a corner, perhaps up against the whiteboard, a place of safety. However, that is (typically) what you least want to do! Here are some suggestions for using the space to show that you are in charge:

- *Stand proud:* No matter how bad you are feeling, try not to let your body show it. If you can manage to stand up straight and proud, you will be demonstrating your high status in relation to your students. Stand tall and you will be 'above them', both literally and metaphorically.
- *Keep moving around:* If your class is badly behaved, you may feel tempted to stand in a corner with your back to the wall, protecting yourself from the worst vagaries of your students. If you can force yourself to keep moving around, you are far more likely to spot those secretive plans for misbehaviour that are being hatched at the back of your classroom. You will also keep your students on their toes because they will never know when you might be approaching from behind them!
- *Vary your levels:* If a teacher always stands upright, and above their students, they are communicating the subtle message that they feel superior in status to the class. *'Hang on a sec! That's exactly what I want to communicate, isn't it?!'* you might say. However, by varying the levels at which you stand, you can show your students that you are extremely confident about your ability to keep control, because you have no fear of coming down to their level. When you talk

to an individual, get down beside them, crouching next to their chair or sitting beside them on the floor. You will also be able to communicate with them much more effectively by doing this.

- *Get close to the troublemakers:* When we are plotting trouble, the last thing that we want is for someone to find out. If you can get close to the troublemakers in your class, you should be able to stamp out any trouble before it takes hold. For instance, if one student refuses to become silent when you are waiting to address the class, go and stand in their 'personal space' and they will receive a subtle message about your high level of control.

- *Give 'em a shock:* Sometimes, to reaffirm your control, it is useful to suddenly change the spatial aspects of your style. This could mean rearranging the classroom from groups of desks to rows. It could mean clearing the desks away and asking the class to sit on the floor. We have already seen how important consistency is, and the majority of the time, your space will remain constant, but once in a while you can reassert your control over the space by imposing your will on it.

Psychological aspects

It's a war out there, and we need to use every single weapon we have at our disposal. We've explored what you can do with your body, but there are also various ways that you can use psychology within your classroom. Not only is this a way of keeping control over your class; it is also about keeping yourself in a positive psychological state. Ideally, you should feel calm, relaxed, but alert. Here are a few ideas about how you might achieve this:

- *Keep 'em guessing:* Again, although I have already stressed the importance of consistency with your students, it doesn't pay to be too predictable all the time. Sometimes (and do it sparingly) you could make a sudden change in your teaching style. Perhaps you are normally quiet and firm with your students. Once in a while, show them that you have another, deadlier and louder side to you.

- *Turn on a penny:* Along the same lines as the advice above, the teacher who is in control should be able to make a sudden change in his or her entire manner when it is necessary. For instance, you might be having a really good lesson when Jimmy decides to spoil things by messing around. It could prove very effective to suddenly turn to him, say viciously *'How dare you spoil this lesson for my wonderful class!'* and then become 'sweetness and light' again.

- *Convince yourself:* If you can convince yourself, *really* convince yourself, that you are in charge, then you will appear to be so. If you truly know 'where you're coming from' (are aware) and *exactly* what you want (are definite), the psychological battle is practically won.

- *Maintain a psychological distance:* In Chapter 3 we explored the idea of reacting from the head rather than from the heart, thus keeping an emotional distance from the misbehaviour that you encounter. By refusing to become emotionally involved with incidents of poor behaviour, you will retain a sense of psychological distance and consequently a strong feeling of control. At the end of the day, no matter how badly behaved your classes are, it really is not the end of the world. Remain in control of your own emotions and you will prove yourself to be firmly and totally in charge.

Attack and defence

I make no apology for using the metaphor of war again to describe what it is like for a teacher working with a badly behaved class. There are only two options for a teacher in this situation – either the students win, or you do. And of course, the victor must be you! In the classroom, it is the assertive, 'attacking' teacher who will get what they want from their students. But what exactly does an 'attacking style' mean?

An attacking style

Being attacking in your style is not necessary about being aggressive. In fact, you should avoid becoming aggressive with your students, because this will encourage confrontations. Having an attacking teaching style is about asserting your dominance by the use of commands, and by deliberately stating what it is that you want. With the attacking teaching style, you know exactly what you require from your students, and you are determined and certain that you will get it. You *tell* the students what you want, rather than *asking* them. Here is an example to demonstrate what I mean:

Rob is holding a paper aeroplane and disrupting the class by threatening to throw it across the room.

Teacher: Rob, give me that paper aeroplane right now.
    Rob: No.
Teacher: I want you to give me the paper aeroplane right now.
    Rob: It's mine.
Teacher: No more arguing. *[Holds out hand]* Give it to me *now*.

A defensive style

In contrast to the attacking style, if you become defensive in your requests you are far less likely to get what you want. The defensive style is characterized by questions rather than statements. The teacher asks the student to do what they want rather than telling them. If you do have a defensive style, your students will sense your uncertainty and are likely to win the battle! Here is the same example, this time played in a defensive way:

Rob is holding a paper aeroplane and disrupting the class by threatening to throw it across the room.

Teacher: Rob, what are you doing with that?
    Rob: Nothing.
Teacher: Are you sure you're not doing anything?
    Rob: Of course I'm sure. *[He throws the plane.]*
Teacher: But you said you weren't doing anything!!!

What teaching styles are effective?

You will know yourself what type of behaviour manager you can be. There is no point in trying to adopt a strict model with all your classes if you are small, petite, have a quiet voice and hate shouting. On the other hand, you may be able to use the strict model to good effect in certain lessons. In fact, it can be more effective to be able to suddenly turn scary. Keep your students on their toes!

In every school there is, or perhaps there should be, at least one teacher that the students are afraid of. It's all part of the drama of school life. This teacher is often someone in a position of authority, because the higher up the ladder you go within your school, the more automatic respect you will be given. Unfortunately, this is not much help if you are on the bottom rung at the moment!

In the interviews, when I asked the students 'What makes a teacher good at controlling a class?' there was quite a diversity of opinions. I had expected that they would opt solely for the strict style of teacher, someone they were scared of, but in fact they did not necessarily feel that this type of teacher was the most effective manager of behaviour. In Chapter 9 you will find much more information about 'What the students said'. Let's take a brief look now at the two types of teachers that the students identified as good behaviour managers, and some of the aspects of their style:

The 'strict and scary' teacher
We all know an example of this type of teacher. Sometimes they even scare us too! Here are a few of the characteristics of a 'strict and scary' teacher:

- They demand perfect behaviour at all times.
- There is a high level of control over the students, for instance lining up in silence before entering the room, or working in complete silence during the lesson.
- They tend to shout at students when applying a sanction.
- They make frequent use of sanctions to control their classes.
- They impose a sanction at the first sign of misbehaviour.

This particular teaching style has various advantages and disadvantages, both for the students and for the teacher using it:

Advantages:
- The students learn that they *must* behave, or they will be punished. It therefore becomes progressively easier to discipline them, once they understand the tight boundaries being imposed.
- The class is generally well disciplined, and a good deal of

work takes place. Well-behaved students are not disrupted by their badly behaved counterparts.

- The teacher does not have to strive to be in a good, fun mood all the time. They can relieve some of their stress by shouting at the class!

Disadvantages:
- This style is physically tiring for the teacher. If a great deal of shouting goes on, the teacher's voice may become worn out or damaged.
- The teacher needs to be physically imposing for this style to work, or to have a strong 'presence'.
- Some of the quieter, well-behaved students can end up in a state of constant fear.
- There is little opportunity for explorative, creative, or group work, because the teacher needs to maintain the silence for their style to be consistent.
- Although the students will behave for this type of teacher, they are unlikely to actually like them.
- There is more opportunity for serious confrontations to arise. If a student decides to stand up to this type of teacher, it is almost impossible for the 'strict and scary' teacher to back down without losing face.

The 'firm but fun' teacher
This is what I personally would see as the ideal teacher/behaviour manager, although you may well prefer the 'strict and scary' model. The 'firm but fair' teacher was liked by the students, at the same time as having their respect. Here are some of the characteristics of the 'firm but fun' teacher:

- They tell the class what they expect in terms of behaviour right from the start, and stick to these rules consistently.
- They will shout if necessary, but normally do not need to.
- They make the work interesting, and set their students hard but achievable targets.
- They do use sanctions, but will give a series of warnings first.
- They get to know their students on a personal level.

This teaching style has the following advantages/disadvantages:

Advantages:
- The students learn to behave through the application of consistent boundaries. Once they have learnt where the boundaries are, they will follow them without having to be told.
- The class is generally well disciplined, and a fair amount of work takes place.
- This style is more relaxed, and less stressful for both teacher and students. There is far less chance of confrontations arising.
- There is more opportunity for creative, exploratory work.

Disadvantages:
- There is a fine balance between being firm and being too relaxed with the class. If the line does slip in the wrong direction, it can be difficult to retrieve the situation.
- The teacher must be relentlessly consistent in applying the boundaries.
- The teacher must be in a good, fun mood for most or all of the time.
- Some of the less-well-behaved students may take advantage more easily.

Refining your teaching style

Once you have made a decision about the type of teaching style you wish to adopt, there are various ways you can refine your own style further. It might be you are a natural comedian, and you should certainly utilize this aspect of your personality if you possibly can. It could be that you are a large, physically imposing man, and again your teaching style will probably be formed by this (although you could buck the stereotype and be a large, physically imposing, but very quiet and timid man!). Here are some ideas about how you might refine your own particular teaching style:

Be a 'real person'
Students often feel that their teachers are distant from what they see

as 'real life' (and perhaps they are right). The things that are of vital importance to children, such as the latest craze, or the big pop group of the moment, can seem pretty meaningless to adults. However, as we saw in Chapter 3, it is essential that you learn how to personalize your teaching, and show your students that you are a 'real person'. This is especially so if you are a secondary school teacher. Not only are you having to deal with large numbers of new names and faces, but you are also coping with students whose close personal relationship with their primary and middle school teachers has been abruptly broken in the move to the secondary sector.

Through your style, try to make your students feel that you like them, and that you are interested in the things that interest them. Talk to them about their behaviour and involve them in making decisions about the way your class is run (although not too much – you are in charge, remember!). Talk to them too about how their behaviour makes you feel, as this will help them in seeing you as a real person. If you do have a really difficult child in one of your classes, why not get to know them outside lessons, where they are more likely to respond positively to you? It could be that they play football, and you are keen to help run the football club. Perhaps they have a secret yearning to take a part in the school play, and you are a closet 'drama queen'. If you can get them on your side by showing you are human it will make life much easier for you in lesson time.

Have a 'mystique'

Although you want your students to see you as a real person, it is rarely a good idea to give too much of yourself away. After all, teaching is not your entire life, and it is important psychologically to keep a part of yourself secret and separate from your students. In addition, if you can cultivate a sense of mystery about yourself, you will make your students curious to find out more. Make it plain to your students that you have a full and interesting life outside school, one that you wish to keep private. You could let slip brief hints about how exciting your private life is, while still retaining that crucial element of mystique.

Create a reputation

It is always most pleasing to overhear students talking positively about your lessons with their peers. I do think teachers tend to underestimate the power that positive word-of-mouth about their teaching style can have. Remember, our students do discuss us in the playground, just as we discuss them in the staffroom. There are a variety of ways that you can create and enhance your reputation:

- *Stay at a school for a long time:* Although this might not be much use to you if you have only just started work at your school, as time goes by, your reputation (good, I hope) will precede you. Many schools take in younger brothers and sisters of those students who are already there. And I can assure you, they will be discussing their teachers at home before they arrive!
- *Use an unusual lesson or lessons:* An inspiring lesson will not only influence the behaviour of your students for the better (see Chapter 6); it will also help you earn a good reputation.
- *Be an entertainer:* If your students see you as an entertaining, fun and interesting teacher, they will tell their peers all about you. When these students arrive at your lesson, at some point in the future, they will already have positive expectations of you.

Use humour in your lessons

The use of humour, and its positive effects on behaviour, are perhaps underestimated in the teaching profession. After all, if it's Monday morning/Friday afternoon, and you're tired, hungover or just plain cranky, you might not feel in the mood for a stand-up comedy routine. However, in interviews with students, one of the major considerations for an 'ideal' teacher was someone fun, someone who made the work and the lessons seem like light relief.

Along with the beneficial effects on students, humour can also offer you a respite from the tension that may build up in a badly behaved class. If you can learn to laugh when things go wrong, or make your teaching fun for yourself, you will feel a whole lot better.

Use humour when you sanction

If a student swears, either at you or just out loud, they expect to be told off. What they don't expect, however, is for you to ask them (in a deadpan voice of course) *'Do you know what the word "****"* *actually means?'*. Surprisingly often, students don't actually know why the swear words they use are offensive, or what their literal meaning is. This applies particularly to younger students, trying to ape their older counterparts. They may simply have heard these words used in the playground (or the classroom), and picked up on the effect that using them achieves.

If you ask this question in a deadly serious way, you will probably find the rest of the class start to laugh. They will be laughing partly at the student's (probable) embarrassment, but also at the sound of hearing a teacher use a swear word. By putting the word in verbal speech marks, and simply quoting what the student has said, you are of course not actually swearing. On a more serious note, by confronting the behaviour, and the problems with it, the student is forced to consider why they should change. They are also made to realize the impact on other people that hearing these words can have.

Similarly, you can dissipate the threat of a personal insult by simply agreeing with what the student has said to you. Hard as it is to react calmly when you are feeling hurt or offended, this technique turns the insult around by refusing to acknowledge its impact. So, when a student says, *'Your hair looks really stupid like that, Miss'*, you could simply answer, *'Yes, I know, and I'm going to sue my hairdresser!'*.

In the same way, if a student makes a statement about your personal life, just agree with whatever they are saying, however outrageous it might be. In this way, they will never know whether you are genuinely agreeing with them, or simply 'taking the mickey'.

Maintaining a positive style

What is a positive style?
Remember that teaching is not just about dealing with badly behaved students, it should also be about developing a relationship with the 'nice' students in your classes. As well as making your life easier, because you are interacting with students who actually want to learn and who behave, it will have an impact on behaviour as a whole within your lessons. If you can get the critical mass of students on your side, it could be that they will influence the

behaviour of the few remaining troublemakers, who will feel like the odd ones out.

By having a positive approach, you will retain your sense of humour and your sense of perspective. If you can achieve this, you are less likely to get stressed when things do go wrong. Learn to see everything that happens in your classroom in a positive light rather than allowing it to make you become cynical and bad tempered, and you will achieve a positive style.

What is a negative style?

A negative approach is all about seeing the worst in your class, in your students, in your job! When things are going badly in the classroom – chairs are being thrown, your students are ignoring you and they simply won't be quiet – it is all too tempting to become defensive with them. The tension builds up inside you, even before the class arrives at your lesson, and you start to expect the worst from them. More often than not, this becomes a self-fulfilling prophecy. Do try to avoid becoming defensive with your classes. For a start, not every single student in a class will be behaving badly, no matter how much it feels like they are.

How do I stay positive?

Here are some ideas that you could try to help keep your style positive:

- *Focus on what's going right:* When there is misbehaviour in your class, it is easy to focus in on this, and forget about all the things that are going well. Sometimes the best way to deal with a troublemaker is to totally ignore them, provided their behaviour is not affecting the rest of the class. Praise a student for good work, and show that this is the way to get your attention, rather than allowing poor behaviour to distract you.
- *Keep yourself fresh:* Teaching can be exhausting, especially if you get involved with lots of extra curricular activities. Do ensure that you don't get too tired, and this will help you keep your style fresh and positive.
- *Don't become defensive:* As I've said before, no matter how hard it is, do try not to become defensive when faced by bad

behaviour. It is all too easy to slip into a frame of mind where you see everything in the worst possible light. React from your head and not your heart, and don't allow the odd incident of misbehaviour to cloud your whole style.

Adapting your style

Teachers who are good managers of behaviour adapt their style to fit their students. Whatever level you teach at, over the years you are going to meet children of a wide range of ages. If you are a secondary school teacher, you will need to learn how to adopt a suitable style for students of different ages throughout each day. The experienced manager of behaviour uses a very different style with a group of Year 7 students and a class of Year 11 students, or a nursery class and a group of Year 3s.

Generally speaking, the younger your students are, the more a 'strict and scary' approach works. To be blunt, younger students are more likely to fall for the fiction of teachers being scary. As they get older, our students start to see through this illusion, and they start to challenge adult authority, testing the boundaries that are set for them.

5 Using sanctions and rewards

Why use sanctions and rewards?

We sanction and reward our students to achieve better behaviour in the classroom. Sanctions offer us a way of forcing our students to work within the boundaries we set them. If they do not do 'X' in terms of behaviour, then the result will be sanction 'Y'. Similarly, we reward our students to encourage them to work and behave as we want, again within the boundaries that we have set. The 'carrot and stick' analogy is useful here. We all respond better to encouragement than to punishment. It is of course up to you to decide how much you want to use the 'carrot' and how much the 'stick'!

Some students do not respond well to either sanctions or rewards. It could be that they are unused to receiving rewards at home, and that they are all too used to unfair or harsh punishments. If this is the case in your classroom, why not focus on giving rewards and sanctions to 'middle' students who will respond well to them, and who can sway your whole class's behaviour one way or the other.

Some thoughts on sanctions

Using sanctions can be a surprisingly complicated business. On the face of it, you should stick closely to the school behaviour policy, or your departmental rules. However, flexibility is the key to good behaviour management, and it is essential that you work out what punishment suits specific students and particular classes. It is also preferable to avoid confrontation with your students, but how on earth are you supposed to punish them without creating conflict?

In addition to this, you should also work out what sanctions you are willing to apply and follow through. As mentioned before, when you apply a sanction, it is essential that it is completed. Although a detention can be a very effective sanction, it can also be very time consuming if the students do not turn up. You are then forced to chase them, and the time this takes means that a brief moment of poor behaviour in class can turn into a cat-and-mouse game of epic proportions.

Sanctions can create quite a negative atmosphere if they are applied too rigidly, and you might also like to consider whether you should be using sanctions at all. In a very difficult school, it might be that you should focus on developing positive relationships with your students, rather than creating confrontation by imposing frequent punishments.

Types of sanctions

There are various types of sanctions that you can use to help you control behaviour in your classroom. In my experience, schools tend to be fairly similar in the types of sanctions that they use. As you will see in Chapter 9, your students can be fairly dubious about the effectiveness of some of these punishments. Much will depend on the ethos of your department, or your school, and on how seriously the students actually take the sanctions.

- *Shouting:* Although not traditionally viewed as a 'sanction', shouting is the most immediate form of punishment you can use with your class, and it is no wonder that so many teachers resort to it. In fact, having a good shout can sometimes be an effective way of letting off steam. Some students seem to respond better to a teacher who shouts than others. However, if you are dealing with a group of extremely poorly behaved students, shouting may be entirely counter-productive. One useful tip about shouting is to do it when you are *not* feeling angry. In this way, the students will realize that you are not letting your emotions get the better of you, but you are making a conscious decision to use shouting to sanction them.
- *Detentions:* Again, depending on the type of students you are teaching, detentions may work very well, or they may be of no use at all. As mentioned before, it is essential that you follow up any students who do not attend your detentions.

If you are not willing to do this, then simply don't give out any detentions. Instead, find yourself another sanction to use. When you give a detention, why not create a punishment to make the sanction more effective, such as collecting plates in the dining hall, or picking up rubbish in the classroom or corridor. This will increase the sense of punishment for the student, discourage them from earning the sanction again, and also improve the school environment.

- *Phoning/writing home:* Never underestimate the power of parents! If you are working with parents who are genuinely supportive, then phoning or writing home can be an extremely effective punishment. If, however (as often happens with badly behaved students), their parents simply do not care, or can't control the child themselves, then this sanction is not going to be all that effective.

- *Whole class sanctions:* In some situations, you may find that a whole class sanction is appropriate, for instance with a class whose behaviour is not particularly bad, but who are very talkative or lively. However, in interviews, students explained how negative they felt about the use of whole class sanctions. They viewed them as unfair. My suggestion would be that, if you do decide to apply these sanctions (for instance a five minute detention for the whole class), allow the class to 'claw back' the time for good behaviour. By doing this, you will probably find that you can avoid having to apply the sanction at all.

- *The 'ultimate' sanction:* Many schools now have a final sanction whereby a student who is causing excessive disruption, or who is posing a danger to themselves or to others, can be removed from the classroom by a more senior teacher. The knowledge that you have this sanction available to use gives the teacher a feeling of safety and reassurance. It can also be useful as a way of enforcing good behaviour, as long as you don't threaten it frequently but never use it. This type of punishment is generally meant to be used as a last resort, although teachers should never be made to feel embarrassed about applying it. There is more information about the 'ultimate' sanction in Chapter 11.

How to apply sanctions

When you apply sanctions, you should always try to do so in a non-confrontational way. As we saw in Chapter 1, you should give a series of warnings, telling the student that *they* are forcing you to give the sanction. By explaining that it is their bad behaviour that has earned them the punishment, you will avoid having a personal stake in sanctioning them. Do try also to give sanctions quietly, without allowing the rest of the class to act as an audience. This will ensure that the troublemaker does not receive the 'oxygen of publicity'. It will also help avoid a confrontation building up, where a student is embarrassed to be punished publicly, and responds by 'taking you on'.

In the first chapter we looked at a brief example of how a teacher might apply a sanction in a positive or a negative way, and the different reactions that they might expect. Remember, when giving a sanction, you should:

- *Keep the sanction private:* As I mentioned above, if at all possible it is very helpful to sanction students in a quiet, individual way. You could ask the student to step outside for a moment to talk with you, or take them to the back of the room where you can discuss the situation with them quietly.
- *Make the situation clear:* As we have seen, misunderstandings can often lead to unnecessary confrontations, so always make your position clear, using repetition as much as possible. State your expectations clearly, telling the student exactly what you want from them, then clarify how the student's behaviour is failing to meet your expectations.
- *Make your feelings clear:* Explain very clearly to the student how their behaviour is making you feel, and how it is impacting on your lesson, and on the learning of the rest of the class. By doing this, you will force the student to see how other people view their behaviour, and consequently why it is so unacceptable.
- *Explain why the behaviour is unacceptable:* Students will often accuse a teacher of being unfair when they give sanctions. By explaining exactly why the behaviour is not

allowed, you are being fair to the student, and also forcing them to look at their behaviour rationally.

- *Offer a positive alternative to misbehaviour:* Sometimes, students back themselves into a corner when they misbehave, and it is up to the teacher to offer them a way out. By telling them about a positive alternative to what they are doing, you may find they accept your offer and the problem is solved.

- *Remember! Repetition is vital:* As we saw in Chapter 3, repetition is vital to make sure you are clearly understood. When sanctioning, keep repeating the warnings you are giving, and use the student's name to ensure you have their full attention.

- *Remember! Tell, don't ask:* As we saw in Chapter 4, the teacher should assert themselves by the use of positive commands, rather than using questions which give the student the opportunity for a variety of responses. Use *'I want'* and *'I need you to'*, rather than *'Could you'* or *'Will you'*. *Tell* your students exactly what you want them to do – they need to know!

- *Give an explicit warning before further action:* After spelling out the situation in the most definite terms, you should tell the student what will happen if they fail to meet your requirements. By giving this warning, you are offering the student a chance to back off from the situation, before you are forced to apply the sanction.

- *Sanction the behaviour, not the student:* Keep the sanction as depersonalized as possible. It should be clear from what you say that the sanction is not a personal attack on the student, but a logical and consistent response to the student's behaviour.

- *Apply the sanctions in clear steps:* Your sanctions should start at a low level, and gradually build up if it becomes clear that the student is continuing to defy you. At each stage, give the student the opportunity to accept that level of sanction, before moving on. The teacher who jumps in with the most severe punishment will be viewed as unfair, and is likely to encourage confrontations.

- *Keep your tone non-confrontational and polite:* Remain relentlessly calm and polite as you apply each level of sanction, however strong the temptation is to let off steam. By doing this, the student will have nothing to feed off and a confrontation is less likely to occur.

- *Offer a chance to 'back out'*: Again, at each stage of the sanctioning process, you should give the student a chance to avoid further punishment. Make it clear that if they accept the current sanction with good grace, and work well for the rest of the lesson, it is possible you may reconsider their punishment.

Let's take a look at two examples of a teacher applying a sanction, to see how the student might react to different approaches. In the first example, the teacher keeps the above advice in mind and avoids a serious confrontation. The second example shows how very differently the situation might have turned out!

A good way to apply sanctions

Carly has arrived at her science lesson in a very bad mood. She is wandering around the room, chatting to the other students. The teacher is ready to take the register and wants to start the lesson.

Teacher: Carly, I'd like a quick word please.

The teacher motions Carly to come to the back of the classroom. Carly follows.

Teacher: Carly, I want to start my lesson now. And I can't do that with you wandering around the room.

Carly: So? What are you gonna do about it?

Teacher: Well, Carly, I really want to get on with my lesson. We're going to be mixing some chemicals together to see if they explode. I'm sure you're really going to enjoy it, but you'll need to sit down first so that I can take the register.

Carly: Oh. That sounds quite good.

Teacher: So, come and sit down, and let's get on with it.

Carly returns to her seat and sits down. Later on in the lesson she gets up again and starts to wander around. Again, the teacher motions her to one side.

Teacher: Carly. I told you earlier on to stay in your seat. I want you to sit down now please.

Carly: No I won't. I'm bored. This lesson is stupid.

Teacher: Well, Carly, I'm sorry that you feel that way, but I'm afraid if you continue to behave like this, and refuse to follow my instructions, I will have to give you a detention.

Carly: That's not fair! I'm not doing anything wrong!

Teacher: Carly. I want you to sit down in your seat and continue with your work. You need to sit down because we're using some dangerous chemicals, and I don't want you to get hurt. Now sit down before I have to give you that detention.

At this stage it is hoped Carly will understand the sanction and why it might have to be given, and will comply with the teacher's request. If she does not, the teacher should apply the sanction, moving up step by step until Carly does as she is told. Now let's look at how differently things might have gone:

A bad way to apply sanctions

Carly has arrived at her science lesson in a very bad mood. She is wandering around the room, chatting to the other students. The teacher is ready to take the register and wants to start the lesson.

Teacher: Carly! Can you sit down please? I want to start my lesson.

Carly: Well, I don't want to start your lesson. Your lessons are stupid.

Teacher: Don't be so rude! Look, why can't you just sit down and let me get on with taking the register?

The rest of the class are watching the confrontation with interest. Carly is now enjoying the 'publicity' of being sanctioned in front of the class.

Carly: No, I won't sit down. Are you gonna make me?

Teacher: Yes I am going to make you. You're in an hour's detention with me after the lesson.

Carly: That's not fair! I'm not coming to your stupid detention!

Teacher: Yes you are. Now shut up and sit down.

The class is getting restless. Some of them are starting to chat and giggle about what is going on.

Carly: You can't tell me to shut up! I hate you and I hate your
lessons. I'm out of here!

*Carly storms out of the room. The rest of the class are now totally
distracted and it takes the teacher another ten minutes to settle them
down.*

Some thoughts on rewards

The use of rewards can be one of the most effective ways of
achieving better behaviour in the classroom. However, indiscrimi-
nate use of rewards that the students are not keen on will not help
you create a more positive model of behaviour with your classes. For
a reward to have real meaning, it must be valued by the students:
they must *want* to receive it. It must also be earned fully by them,
not given for any old bit of good behaviour or work. Using rewards
helps because it shows your students that you are human – that you
would rather use the carrot than the stick.

Some of the best forms of reward run 'close to the wind', and you
will need to decide how far you are willing to go in 'bribing' your
students. For instance, to keep a difficult class focused in the
computer room, it might be an idea to offer them a reward (for
instance, the chance to use the internet) when they have completed
the work set to your satisfaction. Although this is not strictly
'allowed' it can be very effective and it will also win you a reputation
as someone who is open to negotiation. You should of course be
careful that you are not seen as 'easy' by your students.

When using rewards, if you find that a particular reward works
well with student 'X', then go into overload with this reward. For
instance, some students are very keen on collecting stickers, and
there are many excellent types of sticker available nowadays. If little
Johnny loves to get stickers, then give him some every time you can
justify it!

Types of rewards

In my experience, rewards do tend to be very similar from school to
school. This is perhaps a shame, because the many different types of
schools and the students within them respond very differently to the

rewards they are offered. In a school where the students are generally well motivated and well behaved, rewards can be an extremely useful control measure. However, in a school where bad behaviour is the norm, students can appear cynical about receiving rewards. Perhaps the sad truth is that they are scared to appear 'needy' in front of their peers, and a situation arises where rewards are viewed as something to be avoided.

- *Commendations/merits:* In a school where students are reasonably well motivated, commendations or merits can be a good form of reward. Unfortunately, even though this is one of the most commonly used reward systems, it does have its drawbacks. To be perfectly blunt, in a difficult secondary school they simply don't work very well with any year group above Year 7. In today's consumer oriented society, many students need a more tangible reward to strive for. One suggestion that the students came up with in interviews was to have a concrete prize, such as a CD, for those who achieved a high level of commendations each term.
- *Certificates:* Many schools now give their students certificates to reward good behaviour. Again, if your children are motivated by the use of certificates, then they can prove effective. However, your most badly behaved students might not even have a school bag to take the certificates home in!
- *Positive comments:* Verbal and written praise can be very effective, especially if it is done on a quiet, individual basis. We all want to be liked and praised, and I would suggest that positive comments are one of the most effective forms of reward in a school where there is a great deal of difficult behaviour. If you do work in this type of school, your students may be unused to receiving praise, and may react negatively at first. Do persevere, though, until your students see you as someone they want to win praise from.
- *Phoning/writing home:* If your students are keen to please their parents or guardians, then a quick phone call home can really have a huge effect on behaviour, not only for the child concerned, but also for others who want to get this reward too. If you can, catch one of your difficult students on a

good day, promise a phone call home if he or she behaves really well, and start to build a positive relationship with them. In addition, their parents will probably be surprised and delighted to hear something good about them at last!

- *A 'special' reward:* Some schools organize a special event, such as a trip, which can then be earned by the students through good behaviour and other positive contributions to the school. This is an excellent idea, as the reward is tangible, and is also likely to be competed over fiercely. One drawback is that it does require a lot of work to organize this type of event.
- *A special task:* Another idea is to offer an 'adult' task as a reward. Some students are very pleased by a teacher giving them a job that shows trust in them. This can also be useful for you personally. For instance, if you need your stock cupboard tidied, and you can find a student that you trust to do so, this type of adult job will be very effective as a reward. Another adult task that is excellent for motivating students is to ask them to 'be teacher' for a few minutes. They could write up some ideas on the board, or give the answers to a test, while you take a well-deserved break!
- *Whole class rewards:* If you feel your class has been particularly well behaved, a whole class reward can also be helpful. For instance, you might allow your class a few minutes 'chat time' at the end of the lesson. Alternatively, you could create a competition, where the whole class competes in order to win a tangible reward, such as a chocolate bar.

How to give rewards

In a school where rewards are frowned on by the students, they need to be given in a quiet, private way. You could for instance write a positive comment on a good piece of work that only the student will see, or crouch down beside a difficult child who is working well, sharing your positive thoughts about their behaviour with them alone. If you do reward a badly behaved student in front of the class, you could be surprised to find that they do not react well. If a child is unused to receiving praise, he or she may be embarrassed by the attention that you are giving them.

Instead of praising the student during class time, you could always try catching them in the corridor, when none of their friends are around, saying, *'I was really pleased with the way you behaved last lesson, Fred.'* If you do this, you will also show the student that you really care about them, and are thinking about how their behaviour can be improved, even outside the classroom environment.

6 Planning for behaviour management

Why plan for good behaviour?

Planning is an essential factor in achieving good behaviour. After all, your students will spend the majority of the lesson time engaged in their work (you hope!). So, in order to keep them interested and motivated, you will need to make the work as exciting and appealing as you can. The students I interviewed were very clear on this point: if a teacher offered them work they felt was fun, they were far more likely to behave well.

However, there is a subtle balance between what students view as fun activities and what you feel is educational. In fact, there may be a wide gulf between the two viewpoints. After all, given the choice, many children would decide to spend all day every day playing computer games, or out on the football pitch. You, of course, are required to teach them the National Curriculum, and it can be difficult to make some of the material you must teach stimulating, while still covering all areas of your subject.

How to plan for good behaviour

Planning for good behaviour should be relaxing and enjoyable for the teacher. It requires you to use your imagination, and perhaps to spend a little longer on planning than you might normally do. However, this is time well spent if it means you can look forward to better behaviour in your lessons. How, then, do you plan lessons that will encourage your students to behave? Here are some ideas:

- *Make the work fun:* Making work fun can be time consuming when you are planning your lessons. For instance, you might decide to create a board game to teach your students about an aspect of the maths curriculum. However, this could take you a long time. Students tend to view lessons as fun if they seem as little like work as possible. A quiz (as opposed to a test) is an easy and entertaining way to check your students' understanding of a topic.

- *Make the work topical and relevant:* As we have seen, if you can match the work to your students' interests, they are far more likely to be well motivated and take it seriously. Obviously, you cannot achieve this all the time. There will be times when you must teach a particularly dull aspect of the curriculum. However, if you can find out what your students' current interests are, and somehow incorporate them into your lessons, then you will achieve much better behaviour. For instance, at the time of writing, the Pokémon craze is reaching its height. Why not use the cards idea in your lessons? If you are teaching the history of the Royal Family your students could create special Pokémon cards for each of the kings and queens, drawing pictures and giving data about them, just as the cards do.

- *Keep the lessons varied:* If you do have to teach a section of the curriculum that is teacher-led, do follow it with a chance for some group or project work. By keeping your lessons varied, your students will not view your subject or your lessons as dull and repetitive.

- *Keep the tasks short and focused:* The tasks within the lesson should also be as varied as possible. For instance, you could start your lesson with a brief teacher-led explanation of the topic, then follow this by some group discussion and some individual writing.

The importance of time management

The way that a teacher controls time in the classroom can have a surprisingly positive or negative effect on behaviour. If your lessons feel rushed, your students will become stressed and are more likely to misbehave. You should be aiming to achieve a calm, measured approach, where each task has a suitable quantity of time allocated to it. Teachers do often plan to do far too much during a lesson, and consequently find themselves rushing to fit everything in. Try to be flexible about what you can achieve within the lesson time. If your students are badly behaved, it is likely that you will have to spend some of the lesson sanctioning them, leaving you less time to complete the work.

The beginning and end of each lesson are times when you can feel the need to rush to get started or finished. However, when aiming for perfect control of behaviour, these are times of crucial importance. Spend whatever time is necessary bringing your class into your room and settling them down. Some classes respond well to a 'quick start', where the teacher plunges straight into the lesson, while others need time to settle and get themselves in the right mood for work. Again, plan your lessons so that you leave enough time at the end to finish calmly, perhaps factoring in an opportunity to reflect on what has been achieved during the lesson.

Guaranteed to succeed

Some days you will not be in the mood to cope with the difficult classes that you might have to teach, and it is on these occasions that you need some lessons guaranteed to encourage good behaviour. The suggestions below are for lessons practically guaranteed to succeed even with the most difficult students/classes. They have worked for me in a variety of schools, from the 'fairly easy' to the 'downright impossible'!

- *The computer room:* For some reason, putting a student in front of a computer will make even the most badly behaved work well. Many, if not all, subjects in the curriculum offer some opportunities for using computers. In fact, teachers are currently being encouraged to develop the use of IT in the classroom. Why not use this fact to your advantage?
- *Show a video:* Even the most terribly behaved classes will usually sit fairly quietly to watch a video related to the subject they are studying. Frame this as a 'treat' that the class have earned because of recent good behaviour. Do make sure the video is relatively up to date, and interesting enough to keep your students' attention for the relevant length of time.
- *Use an 'engaging lesson':* See the section further on in this

chapter for more ideas about engaging lessons. A lesson that will engage your students will usually offer them something different, something unusual, something adult, and something with 'props', such as the crime scene described below. Although these lessons take quite a lot of planning, they will certainly make your life easier during the class time.

- *Bring in an outside helper:* In my experience, students respond really well to people who are not teachers. Perhaps they are too used to seeing us every day, to hearing our voices and suffering the punishments we give them. If you can organize someone to come in from outside, for instance a theatre group to perform a play they are working on, a police officer to talk about drugs, or a parent to discuss careers, you'll earn yourself a nice easy 'lesson off'.

Behaviour in your age range and subject

I'm an English and Drama teacher, experienced in the secondary sector, although I originally trained to teach 3- to 8-year-olds. You might be a nursery/reception teacher, with an interest in PE, or you could be a middle school teacher with a specialism in science. Clearly, there will be specific behaviour problems associated not only with your age range, but also with your subject interests. The ideas I give in this chapter aim to deal with some of these problems, and also to offer you suggestions for achieving better behaviour, whatever your subject or age range.

Subject-specific problems

Some areas of the curriculum create their own specific problems connected to behaviour. For instance, PE and Drama teachers will probably be working in a large open space, and the lack of physical boundaries can create particular difficulties in controlling disruptive students. In addition, teachers of these subjects will have to deal with lots of noise in their lessons.

Some of the more 'peripheral' subjects in the curriculum can be hard ones to teach. If the subject is not seen as relevant by your students, you may find them misbehaving more frequently. Even the most poorly behaved students tend to see the core subjects of

Maths, English and Science as important. Their parents will probably have told them that they must at least achieve good results in these areas. Unfortunately, they may have an entirely different view of RE or Modern Languages! If and when you do teach a subject that the students see as irrelevant, you will have to try even harder to engage them. Why not try some of the ideas in the following section to see how they work?

'Engaging' lessons across the curriculum

In this section, I'm going to give you a few ideas that I have used, or seen used, to engage a difficult (or even an easy) class. Some of these suggestions might seem a bit bizarre, but remember, if your students are not well motivated in school, the craziest ideas might help to engage them. And in addition to this, you can have some good fun! For each idea, you are given some of the curriculum areas that the lesson might relate to, the requirements for teaching the work, and a description of what actually happens in the class.

The scene of the crime
Possible curriculum areas:
- History (examining evidence).
- English (literature, e.g. *Romeo and Juliet*).
- Drama (the crime genre).
- Design Technology (drawing a plan).

Requirements:
- An open space (could be the middle of a classroom with the chairs pushed aside).
- 'Police tape' or some other barrier around the crime scene.
- Various props that relate to the crime which has been committed.

Description:
Originally used for a Drama lesson, this one grabs the attention of the most rowdy class. You should find that your students quite readily go along with the 'fiction' of the lesson. When they enter the room, the students are told that there has been a crime. They must

not touch anything (they will want to) – ask them why and they'll tell you all about fingerprints!

The class examine the crime scene, discussing their findings and then, depending on the subject, drawing/writing or otherwise responding to the stimulus.

The can of dog food
Possible curriculum areas:
- Design Technology (packaging).
- Art (designing a label).
- Media (the power of persuasion).
- Science (analysing the contents of the tin).

Requirements:
- An empty can of dog (or cat) food (preferably well washed!).
- Mars bars (chopped up).
- Jelly.
- A fork.

Description:
Originally used for a Design Technology lesson, this one shocks the students into paying attention. Once the class is in the room, the teacher shows the students the can of dog food, and then proceeds to eat from it! You may find quite a lively reaction to this, but your students should soon quieten down to hear what you have to say about the disgusting taste!

The class can then examine how we believe what we see on packaging, or test the contents of various cans to see what they actually contain.

The market
Possible curriculum areas:
- Modern Foreign Languages (vocabulary).
- Maths (money, prices, adding and subtracting).
- Art/Design Technology (planning and mapping).
- Drama (character work, improvisation).

Requirements:
- 'Market stalls' (could be classroom tables).

- Food or other goods for the stalls.
- 'Money'.

Description:
This lesson was originally used for a French lesson, where the stalls sold different types of French food, and the students had to go around and buy them using the correct vocabulary. The students responded extremely well to the idea of buying tasty croissants and then getting to eat them!

The lesson could be adapted so that the stalls sell any type of object that relates to the subject, or to the resources that you have available. After visiting the market, the class might draw a plan of where the stalls were, or the entire lesson could be a drama improvisation with the students acting out various scenes at the market.

Using resources

As we have just seen, students do respond very well to resources in general, and especially those that are 'out of the ordinary'. The more resources you can bring into your classroom to use, the more you will find the behaviour of your students improving, and the strength of your reputation developing! Resources come in many different shapes and sizes, and it is often unexpected resources that have the most positive results. Remember that resources are not just objects that you bring into the classroom; they can also be other people. As we have seen, students respond well to someone who is not their usual teacher. Why not ask another teacher to come into your classroom to impart some specialist knowledge, or some students from higher up the school to come and work with your students on their reading?

Part Three

The Students

7 Why do students misbehave?

The reasons for student misbehaviour

There can be a tendency for teachers to think that misbehaviour is planned or premeditated by their students. It is after all only natural, when a well-planned lesson starts to go wrong, to become defensive. You put a great deal of hard work into planning and teaching your lessons. Why on earth, then, don't your students appreciate this? Surely, you start to believe, they have ganged together beforehand and decided to disrupt your lessons? And the belief that they're 'out to get you' can quickly develop into a defensive teaching style.

Whilst it is certainly true in some cases that students make a conscious decision to misbehave, in reality the majority of poor behaviour stems from very different factors. If, as a teacher, you can understand some of these causes and learn ways to deal with them, you may be able to avoid becoming defensive. If you can prevent a negative emotional response in yourself to misbehaviour, you can avoid setting up a situation where confrontations occur between you and your students.

Much of the emphasis in behavioural theory seems to be biased towards making teachers aware of emotional and psychological factors within their students (and within the teachers themselves) that lead to incidents of poor behaviour. You can find more information about dealing with students with special needs in the next chapter. However, whilst it is obviously extremely important for us to know about dealing with the behavioural problems that our students have, there is surely more to the current levels of misbehaviour than this?

In reality, I believe a large part of the truth behind misbehaviour lies outside the teacher's direct control, and within the school system as a whole. Whilst individual teachers cannot really change the education system that they work in, you should certainly be able to minimize the impact of some of these factors. In addition, if you are aware of external factors that cause your students to misbehave, you are less likely to blame yourself for what goes wrong in your classroom, and thus you will be less stressed as a teacher. I have given some ideas below about how you might do this.

School and learning

Boredom

School simply doesn't suit some people. If you think back to your own schooldays, you must surely remember times when you were bored out of your mind. If a student has been taught that school is important, and learning a vital tool for future life, they will put up (on most occasions) with this feeling of boredom, without resorting to bad behaviour. However, if a child has learned to see school as a trap, a place where they are forced to stay despite their lack of interest, it is likely that they will misbehave when they are bored, either to dissipate the feelings of boredom, or to add some interest to the lesson time.

Dealing with boredom

How, then, do we deal with students who are bored by school? The obvious answer would seem to be by making school more interesting! If I think back to my teaching practices at college, I can remember having plenty of time to plan exciting and interesting lessons to engage my students. However, things are not quite so easy for the practising teacher, who has so many other demands on their time. It therefore becomes a question of priorities – if you know for a fact that your students have a low level of concentration, and succumb easily to the temptations to misbehave that boredom creates, then you will need to make 'dealing with boredom' one of your main concerns. Here are a few ideas about how you might do this. These ideas were explored in more detail in the previous chapter on 'Planning for behaviour management'.

- *Make the work fun and interesting:* If you can fool your students into viewing the lessons as fun, rather than as work, they are less likely to become bored, restless and disruptive. The requirement for fun work was right at the top of the students' agenda in the interviews (see Chapter 9 – 'What the students said').

- *Make the work relevant and topical:* A large part of boredom is to do with seeing the work as irrelevant. If you can relate the work you do in lesson time either to jobs that your students might have after they leave school or to topics that interest them personally, then they are likely to stay focused. In addition, if the lessons are topical, for instance if they relate to a current event, or type of music, or news issue, then again the students will view them in a more positive way.
- *Use lots of variety in your lessons:* Students with a low boredom threshold generally find it hard to focus on one specific thing for any length of time. By keeping your lessons varied and giving them lots of different things to do, you should be able to keep the dreaded boredom at bay.
- *Keep the tasks short and focused:* Again, if your students lack the ability to stick at any one thing, you will help yourself by keeping the individual lesson tasks very short and specific. In this way you can also offer praise when each task is finished, or a reward of some type to encourage them further.
- *Offer a 'get out' clause:* Sometimes, a student who is extremely restless and easily bored, will need a 'get out' clause, for when they are having a particularly bad day or lesson. What this means is, you could offer them a deal. As long as they finish 'X' during the lesson, they can have a reward of some type, such as a short break at the end of the class time.

Lack of motivation to learn
There is a difference between a student who is simply bored by school and a student who lacks motivation in their work. Some students lose their motivation because they find the work too difficult, perhaps because they have a specific learning problem. If we can match the work more closely to the student's abilities, then we will perhaps be able to re-motivate them. Other students lack

motivation to learn simply because they have never been taught that learning is important, or that it can be fun.

Dealing with lack of motivation to learn

There are many ideas in this book about how you can make your lessons fun, interesting and engaging. Look particularly at Chapter 6 – 'Planning for behaviour management'. And if you can achieve this, you might be able to turn your students back on to the whole idea of school, and of learning – a wonderful achievement for any teacher! Here are a few more ideas about how to deal with a demotivated student or class:

- Make the learning that will take place in the lesson very clear, by stating your aims at the start of the lesson.
- Make the reasons for the learning very obvious, perhaps by connecting what happens in class to a job that the student might do after school.
- Divide the lesson into individual tasks and set targets for exactly what the student must complete.
- Offer rewards for completing each part of a learning task, to encourage the students to see education as rewarding.

Lack of interest in the subjects

It is a fact that some students are simply not interested in some of the subjects they are taught. Perhaps the subjects don't seem relevant to them and their experience of the world, or perhaps they have a lack of aptitude for certain areas of the curriculum. This fact is increasingly being recognized by the creation of schools which place a particular emphasis on one area of the curriculum, such as Technology, or the Arts.

Dealing with lack of interest in the subjects

Try to discover exactly what your students are really interested in, and if possible use these areas of the curriculum to deliver your subject(s). For example, if you teach French, and your students are fascinated by computers, you could spend some lesson time creating menus, or postcards, or a vocabulary book, on the computer. Similarly, if you teach History, and your students are keen on Drama, you could recreate the living conditions from a particular period in the past and ask your students to 'live' as people of that time.

The students

Special needs

Special needs are of course an important factor in poor misbehaviour, and not just for those students with a specific emotional or behavioural difficulty. As we saw in Chapter 2, before you meet your students for the first time, you should try to find out who has special needs and how their needs will impact on you as their class teacher. If a student does have a specific learning difficulty, for instance with writing, it is your responsibility to know about that problem and take it into account. It is all too easy to misinterpret such difficulties incorrectly, leading to misbehaviour which could be avoided by a full understanding. There is more information on dealing with special needs in the next chapter.

Peer pressure

When we find ourselves in a large group of people, our natural inclination is to 'follow the herd', and behave in a way in which we might not behave if we were on our own. Peer pressure is therefore a crucial aspect in student misbehaviour. There is a great deal of pressure on young people to follow their friends, to win the approval of those who work alongside them. By misbehaving, students can achieve a great deal of positive reinforcement from their peers. If they manage to make the whole class laugh at the teacher, this gives them a great deal of status within the group. There is also a fear that if they don't 'follow the crowd' they will appear to be an outsider and will consequently be open to abuse, such as bullying. It is extremely difficult for anyone, let alone young people, to have the courage to stand out from the crowd. If the majority of the class are involved in misbehaviour, it takes a very strong will not to simply go along with them.

Dealing with peer pressure

It can be extremely difficult, as a teacher, if the bulk of your class is misbehaving. Dealing with one or two incidents of misbehaviour within a generally well mannered group is fairly straightforward –

you simply take the troublemakers aside and 'sort them out'. However, if the whole class is talking, or refusing to co-operate with you, panic can quickly set in, and you can find yourself shouting, becoming defensive, and generally getting completely stressed out. Here are a few ideas about dealing with the problems caused by peer pressure:

- *Impose a whole class sanction:* You need to show your students that peer pressure to behave in a certain way will be punished. You are in charge, and you have a definite idea about how your class will behave. In a situation where the whole class is talking, and refusing to listen to you, try writing your punishment on the board. Eventually a more observant member of the class will see what you have written and 'shush' the others. You could write 'Whole class detention – 1 minute' (and keep adding minutes until they are quiet). An interesting alternative is simply to write 'Do you really want me to set the whole class a detention so that I can get on with teaching my lesson?'. By the time you get halfway through writing that, you will probably find the whole class watching to see what on earth you are doing!
- *Get the 'ringleader' on your side:* In most group situations, one or two individuals are 'in charge'. It will usually be fairly obvious who the 'leader' is in your class. Make a particular effort to get that student 'on side', and you will find that the rest of the class quickly follows their lead. Whilst I am not suggesting that you pander to this individual, you need to find out what motivates their behaviour, and deal with it appropriately.
- *Offer an alternative model:* Eventually, by following the advice given in this book, you will find that your students come to understand that there is an alternative. In the end 'teacher pressure' will win out over 'peer pressure', so do persevere!

Lack of self-discipline

As we grow older, we learn that we must have self-discipline if we are to succeed. We might not want to get up at 7 o'clock every morning to go to work, but we know that if we want the reward of a salary, we must grit our teeth and get on with it. Many of our students may not yet have learned the ability to control themselves adequately, perhaps because they have no tangible reward for doing so.

Some students find it very hard to cope with school because they lack this vital ingredient of self-discipline. For instance, they might be faced with a huge open gym or playing field in a PE lesson, when they have never before had so much space to contend with. It is hardly surprising then that they might run around and test out the new boundaries that are facing them.

Dealing with lack of self-discipline

We need to train our students in the art of self-discipline, if we are going to get them to behave as we wish. Self-discipline and concentration go hand in hand, and all teachers know how important concentration is for effective learning. As a Drama teacher, concentration is one of a number of basic skills that I have taught my students. Here are a few of the exercises that I have used, ones that you could adapt to your own age range or subject speciality. These are known as focus exercises, and if your class is a very lively one, it might be useful to start each lesson with one of these exercises, to settle them down, ready for learning. Alternatively, you might like to end your lesson with some of these activities, preparing your students to go to their next class in a calm state of mind! Focus exercises are essentially a form of meditation, where we focus on one thing for a length of time, blocking out the myriad distractions of the school environment. Here are a few examples:

- *Listening:* Ask your students to close their eyes and listen very carefully to the sounds around them, and outside the classroom. They should listen for a minute or two, then when they open their eyes you can ask them what they heard.
- *Counting:* Ask your class to shut their eyes and count backwards from 50 to 0. When they get to zero they should open their eyes and wait for you to continue.
- *Statues:* In this activity, the students get themselves into a comfortable position and then freeze completely still for a

length of time. You can make this exercise into a test, challenging your class to improve each time. It is amazing how readily students will do this activity. They are, of course, allowed to breathe!

The teacher

Although it is of course entirely unintentional, some teachers (perhaps all teachers!) do contribute personally to their students' misbehaviour. By following the tips in this book, you should be able to avoid encouraging misbehaviour for most of the time. Here is a checklist of 'cardinal sins' you should avoid at all costs. Ask yourself – which of these 'sins' do I tend to commit? If you bear that particular weak spot in mind, you may be able to catch yourself in the act and avoid repeating the mistake in future.

The 'cardinal sins'
- *Winding them up:* Do you engage your classes in lots of frenzied activities, trying to keep them occupied but ending up with your lesson in chaos, and feeling completely frazzled? Remember – staying calm is the key, and this includes keeping your students calm too.
- *Being rude:* Do you talk to your students rudely? Do you use phrases like 'shut up' and 'don't be stupid'? Your students are people too – talk to them as you would to any other adult, no matter how much they provoke you.
- *Being confrontational:* Do you 'take on' your students when they misbehave, battling against them in a tit-for-tat competition of wills? No matter how tempting it is to respond aggressively, you must resist, or you may encourage confrontations that could end in physical violence.
- *Being bad tempered:* Imagine sitting in a classroom faced by a teacher who is constantly in a bad mood. Day after day he or she appears and nags at you, moans at you, complains about the smallest things. And you are forced to sit there and take it. I think that I'd misbehave in this situation – wouldn't you!?
- *Being negative:* Are your first words on meeting your class, 'I hope you're not going to behave as badly as last time?'. If

they are, you may be committing the cardinal sin of negativity. Remember – frame everything you say in a positive light!

How students change

Students in the first year of any school are just finding their way around, getting to know the layout of the buildings, and the way that primary, middle or secondary school actually works. This lack of knowledge about the systems that they must follow means that they are far more malleable, and if you can 'mould' them to your way of thinking and working at this point in their schooling, you may be able to train them to behave all the way through their time at your school. By the time they reach the last year of the school, however, the students are 'on top of the heap'. Their increased status means that they will start testing the boundaries, and incidents of misbehaviour are more likely to occur.

The following descriptions of students at different ages in their schooling are brief, general guides to some of the things that may affect their behaviour. Perhaps we sometimes forget what it was like to be young – to be facing a new school for the first time, or experiencing the confusion that changes in our bodies and our emotions brought us when we were adolescents. If we can think back to these times in our past, we can offer a greater degree of empathy to the students we teach.

The primary school student

When they first start at school, children may be completely overwhelmed by the setting and all the different things that they have to find out. This is often their first lengthy encounter with adults other than their parents, and school can be a confusing and scary place for them. It is no wonder, then, that they might be naughty. In an attempt to test what is acceptable behaviour in this strange, new situation, children may 'act out' in undesirable ways.

In addition to finding the whole new setting strange and confusing, children of this age have little idea of what others think and feel, a very limited understanding of the concept of empathy. It is only as they grow older that children realize that their bad behaviour may make others (whether children or adults) feel unhappy and upset. When I did my first teaching practice at a primary school, I was amazed by how little children of this age actually knew. When I tried to teach a Geography lesson using a globe, my reception class proved to be completely unaware of the greater world around them. All their encounters up to this stage had been on a very local scale, a fact that I had ignored. Remember, then, that school offers young children a very strange and different place to learn about.

The middle school student

Moving from primary school to middle school is in some ways easier than the move from middle to secondary school. In fact, a lot of children will stay at the same school for the whole of their 'primary' schooling. At this stage, children still have only one teacher for all or most of their lessons, and this gives them a sense of continuity. If they do not get on with that one teacher, though, this can be a recipe for trouble! Children of this age are starting to push at the boundaries imposed by adults, and beginning to test exactly how much they can 'get away with'. Puberty is starting at an increasingly young age, and middle school teachers may in fact encounter many of the problems linked to these changes in their students.

Middle school children are becoming more physically imposing, and some of your students may grow much faster than others. It is easy for us to perceive a large, tall child as also being mentally and socially advanced, and to expect better behaviour from them because we expect them to be generally more mature.

The secondary school student

Secondary school can pose many challenges for young people. Not only do they have to adapt to a totally different environment, but they are also moving into adolescence, a time of vast changes in their physical, mental and emotional make-up. Secondary schools are often a great deal bigger than the primary or middle school, both in their physical size and in the numbers of students. It is easy for children to get lost in these new surroundings. In addition to this, before they reach secondary school, children may have many preconceptions about bullying, and other horrible things that they think might be in store for them.

Not only do they have to deal with all these things; they also change suddenly from having mainly one teacher for their subjects to having a different teacher for each one. They will also be expected to move from room to room for their different lessons. Because most secondary school teachers have little or no experience of the primary and middle sectors, it is easy for them to expect more from their students than is perhaps fair. In fact, research has shown that children often 'lose' an entire year's worth of learning in the transition. You can find more information about making the transition in Chapter 11.

8 Types of student

Dealing with different types of student

In this chapter we're going to look at some different types of students, the behaviour problems that they might pose for you, and some thoughts about ways that you could deal with them. There are, of course, as many types of behaviour problems as there are students, because every child is unique. However, by making some generalizations, I believe I can offer you additional strategies to try out with your own class or classes. Before looking at the case studies, which deal with generalized types of behaviour, we should look briefly at some of the special needs that you may encounter during your teaching career.

Special needs

The term 'special needs' has come to encompass a vast variety of different problems that students have. Although not all special needs are directly connected to behaviour, the repeated misinterpretation of a learning difficulty could actually lead to a behaviour problem over time. If a child finds learning very difficult, it is no surprise that incidents of poor behaviour can occur. As a professional, it is your responsibility to cater for children with all different types of needs, from the most able to the least, from the best behaved to the worst. As we saw in Chapter 2, 'Knowledge is power'. The more you know about the needs of the students in your class, the better placed you will be to mould your teaching and your teaching style to suit them.

I make no claims to be an expert on special needs. If you do wish to look more deeply into the causes and treatment of these conditions, there are many texts that you can read. In addition, there will be specialist staff working at your school who know all about special needs. Make sure you turn to them when you are having problems – they will be only too happy to pass on their knowledge. Some of the most helpful tips I have been given for dealing with individual students have come from talking to the special needs staff who work closely with those children. The information given below is taken from my own experience of teaching students with different types of special needs, and the ways I have found useful for dealing with them.

Emotional and behavioural difficulties

This is the big one as far as behaviour management is concerned, and at times it can seem to be rather a catch-all for students who have problems behaving themselves. Students with an emotional or behavioural difficulty may cause problems by being overly confrontational, and unable to control their anger, or they may appear introverted and emotionally fragile. Some of these students will have learned their problematic behaviour through example. Their parents may have reacted in a very aggressive, negative way to them throughout their childhood. On the other hand, some students develop an emotional or behavioural difficulty because of a medical condition.

Dealing with emotional and behavioural difficulties

If you do have a student (or students) with serious emotional or behavioural difficulties in your class, you will need to use all the strategies you have at your disposal to deal with them. The case study in this chapter for 'The aggressive/confrontational student' offers some specific ideas for dealing with one particular individual. Here is some general advice:

- Offer a calm, consistent and positive role model for the student to learn from.
- Greet the student by name at the start of the lesson, and mention your positive expectations of what they will achieve.
- Avoid shouting, as this will only exacerbate possible confrontations.
- Catch the student behaving well and praise them for it. Don't wait for a negative incident to focus on them!

- Set easily achievable targets for work or behaviour that you can reward them for.
- With a particularly aggressive individual, have a back-up plan whereby you can remove yourself and others from danger.

Attention deficit disorder

This is an extreme form of behavioural disturbance, and one that has received much press coverage in recent times. Students with ADD, or ADHD as it is sometimes called (attention deficit hyperactivity disorder), experience severe problems concentrating on an individual activity for any length of time, whether it is undertaking a classroom task, or simply staying sitting in their seat. If you do have a child with this condition in your class, you may find that they are taking medication, such as ritalin, to control the problem. If they do suddenly start to behave in an unusually extreme way, it could be because they have forgotten to take their pills.

Dealing with ADD

If you do have a student with this disorder in your class, you might find they have a 'statement of special educational needs' which enables them to receive additional help. It could be they have an individual helper who works with them in some lessons, or for most of the time at school. The individual case study below on dealing with 'The distracted student' will give you some specific strategies. Here is some general advice:

- As far as possible, ignore minor incidents of misbehaviour from a student with ADD. Focus on them when they are behaving well, praising them as much as you can to encourage them to repeat the good behaviour.
- Focus exercises may help this student to develop their concentration. Look at the exercises explained in the previous chapter – 'Dealing with lack of self-discipline'. Do not, however, expect miracles! A low level of concentration may be all that you can expect from a student with ADD.
- Set small targets throughout the class time that the student

can achieve relatively easily. Heap praise on the individual for every task completed.

- If the student does become completely distracted, or involved in misbehaviour, try to divert them by offering an exciting alternative.

Hyperactivity

Hyperactive children just cannot sit still. This is, of course, a problem in a classroom, where they need to sit still to learn! Hyperactivity is generally a medical condition, which can be exacerbated by certain foods and drinks, for instance those with a high sugar or caffeine content. The advice given above for dealing with ADD will also be helpful in coping with a hyperactive child.

Learning difficulties

There are a huge range of different learning difficulties – with writing, with spelling, maths, and so on. Although a learning difficulty does not necessarily lead to a behavioural one, children can quickly become frustrated and embarrassed by their lack of ability in whatever area. If the teacher responds to a learning difficulty in an inappropriate way, for instance accusing the student of being lazy, then poor behaviour could be their reward!

Dealing with learning difficulties

Your job as a teacher is, of course, to cater for the needs of all your class. If a student does have a problem such as dyslexia, this will have an impact on their learning in all different areas of the curriculum, whenever they are required to read or write. You need to be aware of these learning difficulties, and provide for the individual students in a way that is appropriate to them. Take account of the problems that they may have throughout the class time, not just when they are working individually. For instance, a child with dyslexia may have a problem recording homework or reading from the board. Again, here is some general advice to help you respond appropriately to their needs:

- Find out exactly what the learning difficulties of your students are, and ask the special needs staff at your school for advice in dealing with them.

- Make sure you don't embarrass the student or draw attention to their particular weakness. If you have to talk to them about it, do so in a private, individual way.
- Make some allowances for the difficulty, but keep your standards high. You will not do the child any favours by letting them get away with less than they are capable of.

Special needs staff

There are a wide variety of special needs staff working within education, all of whom will be happy to help you deal with the needs of your students. Depending on the size and type of your school, you may have special needs assistants, educational welfare officers, educational psychologists, and so on working with you, either as permanent members of staff, or as visiting consultants. Do make a point of getting to know these staff. Ask them for help, or for access to detailed information on an individual who is causing you problems. Talk to them on a regular basis, and remember to let them know how well the advice that they gave you worked.

It could also be that you can assist the special needs team in your school by identifying students with a special need that has not yet been discovered. It is often very difficult for the special needs staff to identify new cases of special needs, because they do not teach whole classes on a regular basis. Students may develop a behaviour problem at any time in their schooling, for whatever reason, and you should keep an eye out in your class or classes for students who are experiencing problems, either with their behaviour or with their work.

Some teachers will also have a member of the special needs staff working with them inside the classroom. If this is the case, make sure you plan ahead so that you make the best use of their time. Show them your lesson plans in advance, and if they are willing, ask them to adapt the work you are doing so that it best suits those individuals with particular needs. Find out whether they would prefer to withdraw a few students from the class, to work with on a more individual basis, or whether they feel it would be more appropriate to work within the classroom, helping integrate the students into the mainstream.

Case studies

The following case studies are, of course, entirely fictitious. They are not necessarily about students with special needs, although in each case something is obviously going wrong! As I have mentioned, if you come across some of these forms of misbehaviour in your class, do make sure that the special needs staff are aware of the problems you are experiencing. It could be that the student does indeed have a specific special need that has not yet been identified. For each type of student, I give an example exploring some of the behaviour that you might experience. I also offer a series of suggestions for tackling their behaviour problems.

The lazy/poorly motivated student

Cassie just can't seem to be bothered. She rarely completes any work, and if she does finish something, it is scrappy and of poor quality. Cassie's teacher is torn between just giving up, letting Cassie get away with producing no work, and confronting Cassie about the problem. When questioned as to why she hasn't completed a task, Cassie will say 'I couldn't be bothered, Miss.'

Cassie's teacher has already tried setting detentions to try to get her to complete the work. Unfortunately, Cassie never turns up for them. This seems to be less a deliberate attempt to avoid the sanction, and more because she actually forgets to come.

Strategies for dealing with the poorly motivated student

- Check with the special needs staff that Cassie is not already on their list. It could be that she is experiencing a difficulty with writing, or with understanding your lessons. Ask the special needs team whether she could be tested.
- Set Cassie achievable targets during the lesson. For instance, you could draw a line on the page and ask her to write down to the line in a certain period of time. When (if) she completes each task, give her a reward, for instance some verbal praise.
- If your class situation will allow it, sit quietly with Cassie as she works, talking her through what she needs to do and constantly reinforcing how well she is doing.

- Find out what really interests Cassie and try to incorporate this into your lesson planning.
- Find out what rewards really motivate Cassie. It could be that a quick phone call home when she does work well will result in a beaming face and a hard-working student next time you see her!
- Talk to other members of staff who have taught or who currently teach Cassie. Are they experiencing the same problems? If they are, what strategies do they use? If not, is Cassie only having a problem in your class? If she is, talk to her about why this might be.

The troublemaker

Paul is a nightmare in your lessons! When he does turn up (always late) he immediately disrupts your class by winding the other students up and getting them involved with his misbehaviour. He also acts very aggressively towards the quieter members of the class. He rarely does any work, and when he does complete a task you will find it contains rude, personal comments about you.

When you do try to sanction Paul, he responds very negatively, swearing at you and insulting you. He refuses to attend detentions, and will push past you to leave the room if you try to detain him after the lesson.

Strategies for dealing with the troublemaker

- With this high level of misbehaviour, it is likely that Paul has already been brought to the attention of the special needs team. Check with them about him – is there something specific about his background that you should know?
- It is probable that the rest of the class are also fed up with Paul. Before he arrives at your lesson, talk to the rest of your students about what they could do to help you make him improve. For instance, if they can learn to ignore his poor behaviour, he will have less ammunition to feed off.
- Talk to Paul outside class time about how his behaviour makes you feel, but be careful not to appear vulnerable when you do this. Simply state to him what you see to be the

problem, and tell him that you are going to sort it out, no matter what it takes!

- If at all possible, try to catch Paul being good. Public praise might be useful here, especially if this student responds well to 'publicity'.
- If Paul does respond so negatively to sanctions, consider whether they are in fact worth using in this situation.
- If it becomes necessary, do not hesitate to bring in a senior member of staff to help you deal with the situation. If it has come to the stage where you feel personally threatened by Paul, or where the rest of the class are picking up on his misbehaviour, it could be that he needs to be removed from your class for a while.
- Talk to other staff about their strategies for dealing with Paul. Perhaps he responds well to a particular teaching style.
- If you know that his parents or guardians are supportive, phone home and talk to them about how he is behaving in your lessons. Be careful, though. From the information in this case study, it could be that his parents act in a similar way, and phoning home could make the situation worse (for Paul and for you!)
- Don't take his behaviour personally, or allow it to make you become defensive. Remember – remain calm and relentlessly polite at all times. Never stoop to his level!

The distracted student

Jenna is a nice enough student, but she does find it very hard to stay focused on her work. When she arrives at your lesson it often takes her a while to sit down and settle. When you set a task, she will generally start it off very well, but after a few minutes she will have become distracted, chatting to her friends, wandering around the room, or simply staring out of the window, lost to the world.

When you challenge her about this, she will either promise to go back to work (but fail to) or become upset, and walk out. You have tried various tactics, such as ignoring low-level misbehaviour, or setting her targets to complete, but nothing seems to work. You are concerned that your relationship with Jenna is deteriorating.

Strategies for dealing with the distracted student

- Check with the special needs staff to see whether Jenna does have a specific learning difficulty that you need to take account of.
- Pay Jenna personal attention when she arrives at your lesson, to give her a positive experience of your class right from the word go. Greet her by name and tell her how much you are looking forward to her working well for you.
- Ensure that Jenna fully understands the tasks that you set. After the class has started work, go and sit with her for a while to check that she knows what she is meant to do.
- Set Jenna achievable targets and make sure that you check up on how she is getting on at regular intervals during the lesson. Reward her (with whatever reward best motivates her) for every little thing that she achieves.
- Find out what Jenna enjoys outside of class time. It could be that she is a keen footballer, and would respond well to a sports-related task. For instance, in a Maths lesson Jenna could analyse some data about the number of goals each premiership team scores in a season.
- From the evidence given, Jenna probably has very supportive parents or guardians at home. Give them a call and have a chat with them. If they can support you in praising Jenna for good learning behaviour, then you may well be able to use the offer of a phone call home to motivate her in future.

The student with social problems

Sally is a very strange student. You have seen her around the school, alone at break and lunchtimes, looking very sorry for herself. She arrives at your class smelling and looking dirty, and the other students are forever teasing her about this. Although her individual work is good, she is unable to work well in a group situation. In fact, none of the other students wants to work with her, because her behaviour is so odd. This is putting you in a very awkward position, because confrontations arise within the class when you try to make them accept her into group activities.

When you do talk to Sally individually, she refuses to look you in the eye, and mumbles her answers so that you can hardly hear her. It doesn't seem fair to sanction Sally, because she is not actually doing anything wrong, but the strangeness of her behaviour is having an impact on the class as a whole.

Dealing with the student with social problems

- From the evidence given, it sounds as though Sally needs to be brought to the attention of the educational welfare officer, if this has not already been done. Go and talk to the special needs staff and find out about Sally's background and home situation.
- Try to avoid the need for group work, at least for a while. If you do set a group task, find a way of Sally completing the task individually, but without making her seem like the 'odd one out'.
- Build up Sally's confidence, perhaps by praising her with written comments on a good piece of work. Take care that the rest of the class do not witness the praise, as they may use this as a further reason to isolate her.
- Spend some time talking to Sally individually, gradually winning her trust and getting her to learn how to make eye contact, and talk more clearly. Coax her gently, asking her to try to look you in the eye while you talk to her.
- If the situation with your class seems to warrant it, talk to them without Sally being present about how important it is to accept anybody and everybody when working in a group. Without mentioning Sally by name, ask them to imagine how horrible it must feel to be left out of a group because nobody likes you.
- See if you can find one or two members of the class who might be able to befriend Sally. Try putting Sally in a pair with one of these students to see if she can learn some social skills.

The aggressive/confrontational student

Les is a real problem around the school, and teachers frequently refer to his aggressive and antisocial behaviour in their own class-rooms. He is a large, well-built boy, and you often feel physically threatened by him. At the slightest provocation, Les starts to shout and cause problems. He acts very negatively towards the other members of the class, and they in turn are becoming scared of him.

Les rarely does any work in class, but when you try to sanction him about this he reacts in a hostile manner. On one recent occasion, Les picked up a chair and threatened to throw it at you.

Dealing with the aggressive/confrontational student

- Les clearly has a problem with managing his anger. Again, check that his special needs have been identified and evaluated. Find out from the special needs staff exactly what it is that 'sets him off'.
- Avoid confronting Les at all costs – it is not worth the risk to your own safety to do so, and confrontation is apparently what makes Les aggressive. Instead, try to remain calm at all times. It might be a good idea to tell Les that if he thinks he is going to 'blow', he should leave the room rather than allowing the situation to develop. Find somewhere safe that he could go in these circumstances, for instance to sit outside the school office.
- It is possible that people are reacting to Les's size and physical presence and expecting him to cause trouble. Try to avoid focusing on Les and the problems he creates in your classroom. Only concentrate on him when he is doing something right.
- Ask other staff for advice about dealing with Les, and talk your fears through with a more senior teacher. Explain to them exactly how you feel, and how Les makes other members of the class feel. It is probable that Les's behaviour has already come to the attention of the head teacher, and that he has been warned or even excluded in the past.

9 What the students said

In this chapter we're going to look in detail at what the students said in the interviews that I carried out. All of the students I spoke to were very clear and often extremely perceptive about how their teachers can make them behave. I did find some of their comments surprising, and this is perhaps a reflection of the different perceptions teachers have of students and students have of teachers. I do feel it is extremely important for us to understand how our students view us, and the way that we behave towards them. They are, after all, the ultimate consumers of the educational 'product' that we offer. And of course, if we understand their thoughts and motivations, we are likely to create better behaviour in our classrooms.

The students that I spoke to represented a cross-section of a secondary school community. There was a range of ages, cultural and social backgrounds, and also students who were both well behaved and badly behaved in their lessons. I also interviewed students with a wide range of different abilities. Some were able students who always did well at school; others were less able students, for a variety of reasons; and some had specific learning difficulties.

Classroom control

'What makes a teacher good at controlling a class?'
The students identified two types of teachers who are good at controlling their behaviour. These types are described briefly in Chapter 4 – 'What teaching styles are effective?'. The first kind could be described as 'firm but fun'. This is a teacher who the students like a great deal, but one they know can keep them in line. The second sort of teacher could be described as 'strict and scary'.

Although the students behave well for them, they do not really enjoy the lessons and there was a feeling that this type of teacher did not actually like them. Let's look now at some of the aspects of these two teaching styles that the students described:

'Firm but fun'
- *Teaching style:* This kind of teacher is firm with the class right from the first lesson. They *tell* the class what they expect, rather than *ask* them to behave. (The students identified some types of teachers who they said 'pleaded' with them to behave!) This type of teacher also demonstrates their expectations constantly through the way they discipline the class. For instance they would sort out the students' uniform before even letting them into the classroom. If necessary, they will shout, but they can also be 'nice', 'funny' and 'like a mum' (rather problematic for the male teachers out there!).
- *The work:* This type of teacher makes the lessons and the work seem interesting, so that the students can have fun while they are learning, a point we have already seen is vital. They might also play some games, perhaps at the beginning and end of the lesson. There is a very clear correlation between the students liking a teacher and liking the subject he or she teaches. The lesson is varied and the students are not asked to work in total silence. The students are clear about how much work they need to do to satisfy this teacher – there is work that they *must* do, work that they *should* do, and work that they *could* do. If they are teaching a hard lesson, this teacher will reward the class for their additional efforts. The students felt that it was important that they were not asked to do more than they were capable of.
- *Discipline:* The students know very clearly that this kind of teacher will give sanctions, but that if they do tell their students off, they will do so in a calm and controlled way. If it is necessary to give a 'whole-class' sanction, such as a detention, they will let the good students leave first, so that they are not punished for the misbehaviour of others.
- *Relationship with the students:* The students like and respect this type of teacher; they feel this kind of teacher is always

happy and 'alive'. They feel that they can relate to this teacher because he or she personalizes the work and is happy to chat openly with them. They also feel that this kind of teacher actually likes them, and he or she is always welcoming to their classes.

- *Students' perception of the teacher:* The students explained that this sort of teacher has a good reputation within the school, and this is probably quite an important factor in their expectations and behaviour. They are aware that this teacher has both a 'good' and a 'bad' side and they are wary of getting on the wrong side of them.

'Strict and scary'

- *Teaching style:* This kind of teacher is described as 'strict' and 'scary' by the students, and is more likely to be a male rather than a female teacher, with a strong, deep voice. One student commented that 'everyone does their work but they don't like this teacher'.
- *The work:* The students are expected to complete their work before they are allowed to leave the classroom. At times, the students felt they were too scared of this teacher to ask for help.
- *Discipline:* This type of teacher uses the threat of sanctions to discipline the class, and is also keen on giving out detentions. They will always follow up on a detention that has been set and, if necessary, the students said that they would come to collect you! The students are expected to line up in silence before entering the classroom and, once inside, this type of teacher will often use a seating plan as a form of control – for instance seating the pupils boy–girl alternately.
- *Relationship with the students:* The students used the word 'threaten' quite frequently in association with this kind of teacher. They did not feel that this teacher could ever develop a close relationship with them, or get to know them on a personal level.
- *Students' perception of the teacher:* Apparently, this type of teacher 'looks like they're not scared of the students'. They are given the respect of the students, but this is because of fear rather than admiration.

'What makes a teacher bad at controlling a class?'
Again, the students were extremely clear about what a teacher did or
did not do that made the class misbehave. Much of what they said
referred to the students' perception of the teacher's state of mind.
There seemed to be a substantial gap between what this type of
teacher said they would do, and what they actually did do. This is an
idea that is explored in Chapter 1, particularly in the sections 'be
definite' and 'be aware'. In order to avoid becoming the type of
teacher that the students described, you must 'know what you want'
and 'know what you will do if you don't get what you want'.

- *Teaching style:* This kind of teacher 'acts as though they're
  scared of the kids'. When I tried to pin down exactly what
  the students meant by this, they found it hard to explain,
  but they certainly knew when it was happening. They also
  identified the feeling that the teacher didn't want to get on
  the wrong side of them. Many of the students explained that
  this type of teacher 'shouts, but isn't strict', or is always
  shouting and 'having a go at you'.
- *The work:* The students explained that they behave badly if
  the teaching is not fun, and if the teacher doesn't explain
  things properly. They might do one type of work all the
  time with this teacher, and this results in them becoming
  bored and consequently misbehaving.
- *Discipline:* This type of teacher uses the threat of sanctions
  (for instance, detentions) but doesn't follow through, either
  because they never actually apply the sanction, or because
  they don't chase it up once it is set. Alternatively, they might
  use the ultimate sanction every lesson (for instance, sending
  a student out), becoming over-defensive and giving excessive
  punishments, which the students felt was very unfair.

  The students explained that this kind of teacher starts off
  by being lenient with the class, then if the students
  misbehave they 'plead' with them to behave, rather than
  'telling' them to. They might allow the students to sit where
  they want, rather than using a seating plan. They are also
  likely to scream at the students before they have a chance to
  explain what is going on, perhaps as a result of becoming
  defensive when confronted with bad behaviour.

- *Relationship with the students:* The students were very clear that they want to be treated as equals, and that they dislike a teacher who talks down to them, or who seems to feel that 'you're not as good as them'.
- *Students' perception of the teacher:* The students feel frustrated by a teacher who cannot control them, and one comment was that 'some teachers bring it on themselves'. Another student commented that the class might not even give a teacher a chance, perhaps because he or she is a new, young, or inexperienced teacher. There is also a strong feeling that the teacher who is bad at controlling a class can have favourites, or is seen to treat boys and girls differently. The students also felt that this kind of teacher might 'pick on you', having a go at one individual in particular.

'Describe your ideal teacher'
Whilst there is not necessarily a correlation between what students see as their 'ideal' teacher and a teacher who can control behaviour well, the students I interviewed were very clear that they wanted their teachers to be able to control the class, only they wanted this to be done in a particular way. What the students all described was someone who would fit very closely under the 'firm but fun' style of teaching explored in the section on 'What makes a teacher good at controlling a class?' above:

- *Teaching style:* Words such as 'funny' and 'nice' came up frequently in relation to the 'ideal teacher', who was described as having a 'bubbly personality' and making everything fun. For instance, this teacher might play with words to make the work more interesting. The students also felt it was important for teachers to be 'happy not grumpy', and to have very few 'bad days'. An ideal teacher should also be fairly strict, and have the ability to be serious when it is needed.
- *The work:* The 'ideal teacher' makes the work fun and interesting, and the students were very keen on the idea of rewards for doing their work. The lessons must also be varied, sometimes easy and definitely not always writing, preferably with some sort of games at the beginning and

end. The ideal teacher will also help the students when they need it.

- *Discipline:* Although this mythical 'perfect teacher' can be strict when the class behave badly, they do not shout. The idea that the students had was that the teacher should respond to the way the class is behaving, becoming strict if needed, but staying 'fun' otherwise. The teacher should also give their students a chance before handing out detentions.
- *Relationship with the students:* Again, the students were very firm about wanting to be treated as equals, and indeed why not? They also wanted the teacher to have proper conversations with them.
- *Students' perception of the teacher:* The students felt that they would get to know this type of teacher well. The 'ideal teacher' is firm, but fun, and they would soon develop a good personal relationship with him or her.

Sanctions and rewards

'What punishments work and why?'
The students I interviewed had strong views on how efficient the various sanctions were at making them (and their peers) behave. Overall, they felt that the majority of punishments were useful for the 'good' students, who actually want to succeed, whilst most sanctions are ineffective for the 'bad' students, because they don't care (or pretend not to care) about being punished.

Detentions

The students had mixed feelings about detentions. Depending on why detentions were given, and how they were run, they felt that they were either a useful method of punishment or else a complete waste of time! Some students said that they didn't turn up to detentions, because there was no real pressure to do so. Others said that if they understood *why* the detention was given, they would turn up for it. One or two of the students also said that they had been praised for actually turning up to a detention! Whilst the teacher might see this as positive reinforcement, the students themselves felt it made the detentions less successful.

Another point that students made was that they sometimes felt they were being punished for needing help. Clearly, in this case, the teacher had given a detention for lack of work during class time. However, the student perceived the detention as a punishment for lack of ability. Whole-class detentions were also seen as being extremely unfair.

Short detentions were seen as an effective method of punishment, but long detentions were generally disliked. Detentions given at break and lunch time could cause the students problems, as they then had no time to eat. In fact, I have experienced the difficulties that this can cause; when a student misbehaves in a lesson directly after a break time detention, because they are hungry, their energy is low, and they cannot participate fully in your class. The students felt strongly that the teacher should set them work to do during a detention, or some type of community sanction, such as picking up rubbish. They suggested that this could then lead to a shortened detention.

Being sent out/taken off timetable

The 'red card' system, where a student is removed from the classroom, was viewed as a good punishment, mainly because it got the very bad students out of lessons and allowed the others to continue with their work, uninterrupted. The students were also aware that such a high-level punishment went on the records of these students, which was viewed as a good thing.

However, they felt that being sent out did not have much of an impact on the behaviour of the 'bad' students, because it was viewed as a big joke. (It could be, of course, that the 'bad' students played down their embarrassment at being given a severe sanction by making a joke out of it.) Taking a student off the normal timetable because he or she had misbehaved was also viewed as a bit 'stupid', because he or she had then achieved exactly what they wanted, which was to get out of lessons and avoid doing any work!

Exclusion

The majority of the students I interviewed did not expect ever to be excluded. However, they had firm views about how exclusion was seen by those who did merit such a severe sanction. Whilst they did feel that exclusion helped create a climate for better behaviour in their lessons, I was surprised to find that they also felt exclusion would mean 'a day off school to do what you want' for the most badly behaved students in a school.

Other forms of sanction

The students felt that being put on report was a very useful sanction, particularly if they had to report to a teacher at lunch time. They also suggested that it would be useful to have a meeting with the teacher, the parents and the head if a student was consistently misbehaving. Although many schools do call in parents to talk to the head teacher, it might also be useful for schools to consider including the teachers in such a meeting. The teacher is, after all, the person who must actually deal with the student on a daily basis.

Phone calls and letters home were seen to work if the parents of the student are strict, and many of the students interviewed said that they did try to avoid this sanction. However, the interviewees also pointed out that some parents don't care how their children behave in school, and if this is the case, then the sanction is fairly meaningless.

'What rewards work and why?'

Again, the students were surprisingly unimpressed by the majority of rewards they were given at school. Probably the main 'reward' they actually experience, perhaps without properly realizing it, is verbal or written praise from a teacher they respect. The students were impressively materialistic, suggesting that decent and tangible rewards would be far more likely to make them behave! Happily, some of the most well motivated students did identify the more subtle reward of a good education at the end of their schooling!

Commendations

As we have already noted, commendations or merits become far less effective the higher up the school a student goes. When they first arrived at the school, the interviewees were keen on collecting merits. They did point out, however, that it was mainly the 'good kids' who wanted them, and they were therefore not particularly useful as a form of control. Some of the less well behaved students who I interviewed pointed out that, as they kept losing their diaries (where the commendations were noted), they had no way of collecting them.

The students felt that commendations became less effective because you didn't actually get anything for them. They felt that if you received points for commendations, which you could then 'cash in' for a prize, this reward would seem much more effective. The students also pointed out that some teachers forgot to give them, or that their teachers 'glazed over' the good, quiet children in the class, and ended up handing out this reward to those students who were loud and noisy. This is obviously a mistake, as the students then begin to feel that you only get rewarded if you make a fuss, or if you are a 'loud' character. Something that no teacher wants to encourage!

Awards evening/certificates

For the students whose parents rewarded them for their achievements, certificates were viewed as a very popular reward. The students pointed out that certificates should be given as publicly as possible, for instance in assembly, so that the reward seemed far more tangible.

Other suggestions for rewards

As I have already pointed out, the students wanted a tangible reward for good behaviour. For instance, they could be put on 'desk duty', running errands for the office and for teachers (and missing lessons as a result – a very popular option!). Another popular tangible reward was badges, or prizes such as Mars bars and cans of Coke. What a materialistic bunch we teach!

Other factors affecting behaviour

'What effect does the classroom environment have on your behaviour?'
The students felt that if a classroom was already scruffy, they would be far more likely to drop litter on the floor. If, on the other hand, the class environment was bright and colourful, this made them want to keep it that way. Some of the students felt that the rooms they were taught in were 'dull' and 'cold'. If this was the case, they were less than happy about working in these rooms, and more likely to misbehave as a result.

'What subjects do you find it easiest to behave in?'
Unsurprisingly, perhaps, the students felt it was easiest to behave in the non-academic subjects, such as Art, Music and PE. They explained that these areas of the curriculum needed less concentration, and they felt more relaxed during the lessons. PE in particular was seen as being a fun lesson rather than a work lesson. For this reason, school sports day can be very illuminating for teachers, when they see some of their worst-behaved (and non-academic) students achieving wonderful things.

The students also felt it was easy to behave during form or tutor time. This was partly because they knew the other members of their form well, and thus felt relaxed. In addition, form time was seen as different to lesson time, because they were not expected to work as such. On a more general level, the students explained that in the lessons they didn't really care about, or that they saw as irrelevant, they were more likely to mess around.

Student thoughts on misbehaviour

'What do you feel about very badly behaved students?'
The interviewees had mixed feelings about badly behaved students. Superficially, they found such students funny, and felt that they added interest to the lessons. Worryingly, they also saw a clear relationship between being badly behaved and being popular. The majority of students did not feel personally threatened by the badly behaved people at school.

However, feelings of annoyance were also voiced. The interviewees felt that these students took all the teacher's attention, and this was not fair. They also offered feelings of sympathy for teachers who were faced with bad behaviour. There was a strong sense that these badly behaved students should not be allowed to affect adversely their own education.

Some of the students mentioned that they had been called 'boffins' by the badly behaved members of the school, because they wanted to behave well. As we have already noted, it is hard to stand out from the crowd! This name calling was, however, viewed with derision, particularly by the older students, who explained that the others were just jealous of them, because they wanted to work hard and get a good job. They also said that there was a tendency for boys to call girls 'boffins', and this would seem to back up findings about differences in achievement levels and motivation between male and female students.

'Why do students misbehave?'
Again, the students were very clear and perceptive about why their fellow students misbehaved. They identified the 'ringleaders' whose example they would follow because they were scared not to. In addition, these ringleaders were seen as being popular members of the class, and being popular was viewed as a very important attribute. The students explained that they would follow the 'bad kids' because those people were loud, daring and willing to challenge teachers. Often, this misbehaviour would seem funny to the class, and they would therefore want to 'have a go' too, to see what effect they could create. If their friends were 'mucking about', the students explained that this would make them feel more confident about 'having a go' too.

As we have established, boredom in lessons can be a major factor in creating misbehaviour, and this was something that the students identified with strongly. By messing around, they would get attention, both from the teacher and from the rest of the class. In this way, they would look 'hard' in front of their friends and create a distraction from boring work. Another problem was an inability to control themselves, the problem of lack of self-discipline we have already identified. This lack of self-discipline was stronger at particular times of the day and week, or after particular lessons, such as PE. Perhaps because they had to move from an 'open' environment to a closed classroom, where they were required to sit down, their levels of self-discipline were affected.

The idea of 'gangs' also came up. Those students who were unwilling to join in with a gang in behaving badly expressed the fear that the others might become violent towards them, or turn people against them.

'Describe a badly behaved student'
When asked to describe a badly behaved student, the interviewees listed a number of characteristics:

- They 'backchat' to teachers, i.e. talk to them rudely when their behaviour is challenged.
- They make a big deal out of being given a sanction, even when they have earned it.
- They enjoy showing off, and want to get their own way all the time.
- If they don't get their own way, they might walk out of the class.
- They 'act hard' in lessons.
- They are willing to swear, both at other students and at the teacher.
- They don't care about learning, perhaps because neither they nor their parents care about getting qualifications.
- They are likely to smoke outside lesson time.
- They are also likely to be identified as a bully by other students.

In addition, the students mentioned some more 'positive' aspects related to being badly behaved:

- Badly behaved students get respect from their peers.
- They are more likely to get the teacher's attention.
- They are also more likely to be popular within the peer group.

'What should be done about badly behaved students?'
This question seemed to leave the students rather stumped! One suggestion that they did give was that there should be special schools for naughty children. This would be a good idea, they said, because it would allow the people who do want to work to get on with it. A second idea was that the 'ringleaders' should get 'taken out' (by whatever method) early on. If this happened, for instance in their first year at school, their peer group would behave well, because they would not have picked up on how 'rewarding' misbehaviour could be.

'Do you behave well? If so, why?'
Those students who did consider that they behaved well had a strong motivation (usually from home) to succeed. Parental influ-

ence was cited as a very important factor, along with older brothers and sisters who had gone to university. These students were not afraid to stand out from the crowd, or to be termed 'boffins', because they knew it was okay to be smart. They wanted to do well, and get the best education they possibly could, because that way they could get the job they wanted. Clearly, for our students to be well motivated, it is essential that they understand the link between a good schooling and success in later life.

Making the transition

'How well did you settle down in Year 7?'
Because the students I interviewed were from secondary schools, I thought it would be interesting to find out how they had handled the transition from the primary to the secondary sector. This could also be of interest to the teacher working with students just starting a school at any age. The students told me that they got lost very easily, and found it difficult to adapt to a big, unknown building. They felt very confused in their first few weeks and months at the new school – there were lots of different teachers who all had their own different styles, and this was difficult to adapt to. They also pointed out that there was a very heavy homework load, much heavier than they were used to, and this had caused some students considerable problems. As time went by and they settled in, the students felt they were adversely influenced by watching the behaviour of the older members of the school.

Part Four

The Wider Environment

10 The classroom

The classroom environment

Think for a moment about the way the spaces we live in affect the way that we feel. For instance, if you live in a small flat with several other people, you may find yourself becoming stressed and losing your temper easily. People start to get under each other's feet and feelings run high. Similarly, if you live or work in a cluttered and untidy environment, you are likely to feel depressed and mentally 'overcrowded' as well. If, on the other hand, you are lucky enough to live or work in an open, spacious, light and airy place, with a wonderful view, you are likely to spend your time there in a much more positive mood, and consequently you will live or work in a better, more relaxed way.

The way that you as a teacher use space, and also the way that your classroom is set up, will have a huge impact on the behaviour of your students. In Chapter 4 – 'Teaching styles' – we explored the way that a teacher can use the spatial aspects of their style to help improve behaviour, for instance the way they stand and the way they move around the room. In this chapter we will be exploring how the actual physical environment of the classroom can be used and improved to have a positive impact on behaviour. In addition to helping you control the behaviour of your students, your classroom should also help *you* stay calm, happy and relaxed.

From the moment they first arrive at your room, your students will be making judgements (probably subconsciously) about what to expect from you as a teacher, simply by what they first see of you and your room. You want to create the feeling for your students that this is an environment where you are in control. In response to this, your students will immediately view you as someone who knows how to be 'in charge'. Whilst there is much about our classrooms that we cannot change – for instance, their shape, their size, and often their general condition – there are also many ways that we can improve the 'look' of our rooms and consequently the behaviour of our students within them.

Improving the classroom environment

Your students need to perceive your room as a safe, calm environment where learning is going to take place. If you teach in the primary sector, this is the place where your children are going to be spending the majority of each day, and it should therefore be as welcoming, comfortable and well organized as possible. Similarly, if you teach in the secondary sector, this is the place where *you* are going to be spending the majority of your time, and each class that visits you there should find you in control of a wonderful 'haven of learning'! Here are some ideas about how you can improve your own classroom environment.

- *Keep it tidy:* While it may sound obvious, a tidy environment is essential for creating a tidy style in your teaching. If we are surrounded by clutter, it is much harder to work, for instance if we need to find a specific piece of equipment. If you can, keep all your resources – files, folders, pens, and so on – in one area, so that the room looks tidy at first sight.
- *Keep it organized:* In the primary classroom, where resources for many different subjects need to be stored, it is very useful if you can set up 'stations' for all these resources, and then train your children so that they know where they should go to get a particular thing. Similarly, in a secondary classroom you might have a specific place where your students store their text books and exercise books. You can then instruct them to retrieve their learning materials as soon as they arrive at your classroom, or ask one trustworthy student to give out the books and other equipment.
- *Keep it safe:* Do make sure that your classroom is a safe environment for your students to work in. You are responsible for their health and safety while they are in your room – make sure that those dangerous chemicals or sharp scissors

are kept well away from temptation, especially if you have students whose behaviour is not always perfect! Of course, your classroom also needs to be a safe environment for you to work in. If you do have any concerns about this, there should be a health and safety representative that you can talk to at your school.

- *Make it fun and colourful:* Interesting displays can really add to the sense of a good, positive classroom environment. Displays are also a very effective learning tool, and a good way of celebrating your students' achievements. See the following section – 'Some thoughts on displays' – for more advice about how you could do this.

- *Personalize the space:* You are going to be spending a lot of time in this room, and you also want your students to view it as very much 'your space'. Why not, then, bring a few personal touches into the room? For instance, if you love plants, you could add some greenery to your classroom. Or if you are an animal lover, you could introduce a class pet, something that young children particularly respond very well to. (In addition, you can educate them about keeping pets, and also give them responsibility for taking care of the animal, possibly as a reward for good behaviour.)

- *Think carefully about the layout:* The way you set out the desks in your room will have a strong impact on the way your students perceive your 'style' as a teacher. It will also have an effect on the way your students behave. See the section in this chapter on 'Classroom layout' for some more ideas on how this might work.

Some thoughts on displays

No matter how poor the general condition of your classroom is, you can always cheer it up by the use of displays. In fact, it might be that you can use displays as a good way of covering up dirty walls or peeling paint! However, do not simply view your displays as 'wallpaper' – they must be worthy of their place on your walls! Displays can also offer opportunities to further your students' learning, and are an excellent way of praising the work that they do for you. Here are some thoughts about how to create good displays:

- *Make them interesting:* If you want to use displays to the maximum effect, they must be interesting to look at. This means that you cannot simply stick several pieces of work to a sheet of sugar paper, and chuck it on your wall. If you have access to the resources, use a variety of bright colours on each display. Perhaps you could create a three-dimensional display related to a current topic, for instance you could have 3-d fireworks flying across your wall at the time of fireworks night. Don't forget the ceiling as well as a place for displays – tie a piece of string across your room and you can hang the students' work from it.
- *Make them interactive:* If we want our students to take notice of the displays, they need to capture their attention, and make them curious to interact with them. You could put big questions on the wall, related to the topic you are studying. Or you could have 'lift up' flaps for the students to look under.
- *Keep them tidy:* Over time, your displays will inevitably become tatty. For displays to remain effective, they need to be kept tidy. Replace drawing pins regularly, tidy up any ripped corners, or simply change the display (see below) as soon as it becomes tired.
- *Change them regularly:* When we are under the pressure of time (as teachers usually are!), displays often seem like the last thing we should be worrying about. However, as we have noted, our environment can have a powerful impact on the way we work and behave. If you simply stick up a load of displays at the start of the year, then run out of steam, your students will cease to notice them. Displays should always be connected to the current learning that is taking place in your classroom (see below).
- *Relate them to the learning:* Displays are an excellent way of applauding your students' current attainment. In addition, praise of this type is a good way of reinforcing the positive work and learning that takes place in your classroom (and consequently a helpful way to encourage good behaviour). A display does not necessarily have to be a show of work that your students have completed at the end of a topic; they can also be related to the learning as it goes along. For instance if

you are studying the local environment, your students could create a map of the area to help them during the topic.

Classroom layout

The way that your classroom is laid out can have a strong effect both on your students' behaviour and on their perception of what will happen inside the room. Depending on your age range and the subject(s) you teach, you might have to decide how to set out desks and chairs, or stools and lab benches, or whatever type of furniture you use. There is no reason why you should not change the classroom layout on occasions, depending on the type of work you are going to be doing. In fact, this can be a helpful control strategy (see Chapter 4 – 'Showing who's in charge'). However, if you share your room with another teacher, do make sure you return the desks to their previous arrangement!

Here are some thoughts about how the students might perceive different classroom layouts, and also their possible impact on learning and behaviour. The examples given use the most common type of classroom furniture, desks and chairs, but you should be able to relate these comments to your own particular set-up.

The desks in rows

Having the desks in rows, facing the front, is perceived as a more traditional way of setting up the classroom, both by teachers and by students. It is an option generally favoured by the 'strict and scary' style of teacher (see Chapters 4 and 9). It can also feel like a safer option for the teacher who is having trouble controlling the behaviour of their class.

Advantages: The students are all facing forwards, and it is therefore relatively easy for the teacher to see anyone who is chatting, or who is likely to misbehave. The students can all see the board, and resources, books, etc, can be easily passed along the rows. This type of layout also makes it easier for you to draw up a seating plan.

Disadvantages: It is difficult to do group work with the desks set out this way, and there is sometimes a tendency for teachers to ignore students at the ends of each row, simply because they are out of the line of sight. This type of set-up does tend to favour the 'chalk-and-talk' style of teaching, where the lessons are teacher-led. In addition, the teacher can only work with one pair of students at a time.

The desks in groups
Grouping the desks is generally seen as encouraging a more modern style of teaching, where much exploration and group work takes place amongst the students. For a teacher with a difficult class, this style of layout can be a source of problems, because it is harder to control behaviour when the desks are grouped.

Advantages: Group activities can take place easily, and the class work is more likely to be student based. The teacher can talk to a whole group at a time, and it is likely that he or she will move more freely around the room during the lesson.

Disadvantages: Because the teacher cannot see all the faces, the students could get away with chatting and plotting misbehaviour more easily. In addition, it is harder for the students to see the board. The students may view the teacher as less traditional, or strict, and this perception could also lead to behaviour problems.

Some thoughts on different spaces

Teachers work in a huge range of different spaces, depending both on the age range that they teach and the subject or subjects that they specialize in. Teachers in a primary or middle school will work mainly within one space (their classroom), but they could also spend time in other places within the school. They might work in the school gym to teach PE, or outside in the nature area for a Science lesson. Secondary school teachers are more likely to be restricted to one room (or several different rooms if they are unlucky enough not to have their 'own' teaching space). However, even secondary teachers will at times have the desire or opportunity to move from their normal space to a different one, for instance measuring the school playground in a Maths lesson.

Each of the spaces within a school has its own natural advantages and disadvantages for behaviour management. If we wish to maximize our control over our students' behaviour, we need to be aware of these positive and negative aspects of the spaces that we work in. The ideas below should help you understand these features, and help you exploit the advantages of your own space or spaces, and minimize the difficulties that you might encounter:

The classroom

When dealing with problem behaviour, the classroom space has many advantages. The fixed nature of the seating and desks in the classroom gives a strong sense of control, both for the teacher and for the students. Once the class are seated in their places, there is far less opportunity for them to move around, and consequently less opportunity for physical disruptions. From the front of the room, the teacher can generally see all the students' faces, which helps them to ensure that the students are concentrating fully and behaving sensibly.

On the downside, students seated at desks are physically restricted, and may look for alternative outlets for their energy, particularly if they are restless, or if they lack the skills of concentration and self-discipline. These outlets may take the form of students 'rocking back' on their chairs, or alternatively creating disruption by excessive noise or poor behaviour, such as throwing things across the room. Students who do find it extremely difficult to sit still may get up and wander around the room. The room could also be fairly cramped if it is small, with a large number of desks and chairs in it.

Maximizing the advantages

Because it is helpful for control to have your students seated, this should become a priority in the classroom space, particularly if you are having problems with behaviour. Make it clear from the first time you meet your students that one of your most important rules is 'stay seated at all times'. If they do need your help, the students should be trained to raise their hands and wait, and you will come to them in the order that their hands went up. You might wish to add a rider to your rule, that 'if you do need to leave your seat, you must first have the teacher's permission'.

As we saw in the previous section, having your desks in rows facing the front is probably the preferred method for a difficult class. When you address the class as a whole, make sure that all the faces are turned towards you, and that each student is attentive, and ready to listen. Use one of the phrases from Chapter 3, such as '*Looking at me and listening please*' to get their attention.

Minimizing the difficulties

If you do have a particularly restless class or individual student (and a long lesson time), it could be that the rule for staying in their seats is very difficult to apply. You could set 'staying in your seat' as a target for individuals, rewarding them if they manage to do so throughout the lesson. Alternatively, you could have a brief 'movement' time, perhaps when students are gathering materials for their work, and then a signal, such as clapping your hands, for when you want them to return to their seats. If you do choose to use a movement time, it is a good idea to allow only one group of individuals to go at a time.

The Science lab

Science rooms offer the teacher certain advantages for working with difficult classes. They can be very exciting places for your students to work in, with interesting equipment to use, and fascinating experiments to try out. Science teachers in a secondary school will often have the services of a lab technician to help them prepare their lessons, while the teacher concentrates on controlling and teaching the class. In addition, it is likely that the lab benches will be in a fixed position within the space (probably facing the front), and this means that students cannot cause disruption by moving the furniture around. If the benches do face the front of the room, it is easy for the teacher to demonstrate a practical experiment before the students have a go.

On the other hand, a science laboratory can be a dangerous place to work in. Safety issues must be at the forefront of the teacher's mind, and if you are teaching difficult students, it may be tempting to avoid practical work because of the possible hazards. Labs may also have sinks and taps, which could prove appealing for our less sensible students!

Maximizing the advantages

Do try not to shy away from practical work if you teach Science in a lab. This is just the type of lesson that students see as fun and interesting. It is only through experience that they will learn how to conduct experiments in a safe and sensible way. It could be that you have to suffer a few very stressful practical lessons before your students are properly trained in using the equipment. Again, make sure your class is facing front, looking at you, and concentrating fully, before you address them. You could use the reward of being allowed to do a practical experiment to ensure that you have the class's full attention while you demonstrate exactly what they have to do.

Minimizing the difficulties
As far as possible, keep temptation away from your students. Lock any dangerous chemicals, or tools, in a cupboard, or keep them in another room. Make it clear right from the start that you will not stand for students messing around with taps and sinks, and that to do so would be to incur an immediate sanction. Perhaps you could spend your initial lessons training your students in lab safety, making posters to display on the walls to remind them of the rules.

'Open' spaces
Open spaces, such as the Drama studio, the gymnasium, or the hall, can be wonderful environments for learning. Your students have a greater degree of freedom to move around in an open space, and they are less likely to feel restricted and restless. Lessons that take place in these spaces, such as Drama and PE, tend to be those that students enjoy. They are also generally less academic areas of the curriculum. There tends to be less focus on activities such as writing and book learning, which can lead to disruptive behaviour.

Open spaces do, however, have certain drawbacks for the teacher when it comes to managing behaviour. The sight of a big, open space may offer your students an overwhelming temptation to run around, and it can prove difficult to pull the class together into one place. In addition, there could be a high level of noise during the lesson, and this can make it difficult for the teacher to regain control. If you do wish to do some written work in an open space, you might not have any chairs and desks for your students to work at. Students may also resent being asked to write for these types of subjects, because they don't see them as work, and they may therefore cause you problems if you ask them to do a written task.

Maximizing the advantages

From the first time that you meet your students in an open space, make it clear that the work will be fun and full of excitement. However, you should also make it perfectly apparent that they will need to develop a high degree of control and self-discipline to enjoy your lessons properly. You could use the threat of not doing a practical lesson as a form of control over students who lack self-discipline. If they want to have fun, they *must* learn to follow the rules.

Minimizing the difficulties

From your very first lesson, make it clear to the class how they should behave within the space. You could perhaps line them up outside and tell them that when they are allowed in, they must immediately sit on the floor (in a circle or in a group) so that you can start your lesson. If they fail to follow this instruction, take them back outside and line them up again, explaining to them that they are wasting their fun lesson time. Make sure too that you find a good way of gaining the class's attention within your open space. In Chapter 3 – 'Wait for silence' – you will find some ideas about how you might do this, such as using a silence command.

If you do need to do a written activity with your class, there are various ways you might approach this. You could, for instance, set all written tasks for homework, and only allow the students to do a practical lesson if their homework is complete. Another alternative would be to split the lessons up into a practical session, followed by a writing time. If you do not have any desks and chairs in your room, you could ask the students to sit on the floor and write on clipboards, or you could find an empty room that is more conducive to written work.

Teaching outdoors

Just as with working in an open space, teaching outdoors offers a wonderful sense of freedom for your students. They will also see it as something out of the ordinary, a chance to escape from the school building and explore the wider environment. The advantages and disadvantages of working outside are also very similar to the 'open space' example given above. Remember – explain your behaviour requirements to the class before they enter the space. If you don't do this, you will find it very difficult to regain their attention. Similarly, you should find some sort of silence command that the class will understand and respond to.

The teacher within the space

As we saw in Chapter 4, the way that the teacher uses space is very important in achieving control of behaviour. Your students will look at the way you set up the space, and the way that you move around within the space, and make decisions about how they are going to behave. Here are a few ideas about how you might work within the space to achieve better control of your class:

- *You control the space:* Make it clear from the word go that the space is yours, and that you are in control of it. You will do this by setting up the room as you want, moving around the space in a dynamic way, and also by telling the students how they must behave within the space. In addition, include some personal touches which define the room as your territory (see 'Improving the classroom environment' earlier in this chapter).
- *Surprise them!:* You can surprise your students by changing the way your room is laid out (on occasions), and also by using the space in an unusual way. You might decide to sit on a desk, rather than leaning against the board at the front of the classroom. Or you could decide to stand at the back of the room while you read a piece of text to your students.
- *Think vertically as well as horizontally:* When you are moving around in your room, use up and down as well as side to side to create an interesting use of space. Crouch down beside a student to talk to them, ask your students to sit on the floor to hear a story, or stand on a desk to declaim a poem to your class (think *Dead Poet's Society*!)

Dealing with problem spaces

Many teachers have to deal with a space that causes them problems, and consequently affects the behaviour of their students. You might be working in a very old, run-down school where the paint is peeling off the classroom walls. Or you could have to cope with a gym that is split into two for PE lessons, where only a flimsy partition separates you from the other class, and the noise levels can become horrendous. Or your room might have a huge bank of windows on one wall, making it freezing cold over the winter, and boiling hot in the summer months.

My first ever classroom was the classic 'problem space'. The room was tiny, although I had classes of up to thirty Year 11 students, who would fill the space to bursting point. There were two doors into the classroom, one at either end, and because the room linked two areas of the school together, it was seen as a useful corridor, sometimes even during lesson time! The room was long and narrow and the students had great difficulty seeing the board. There was no room for movement once the classroom was full, and it would become hotter and hotter as the lessons wore on, particularly on summer afternoons when the sun shone straight into the room through windows without any blinds.

At the opposite extreme, I have also taught in a large, open space that caused me problems. This room had terrible acoustics, because of a very high ceiling, and this meant that any noise the students made was amplified tenfold. Because the room was so large, the students' movement was completely unrestricted, and this led to behaviour problems as they ran around the space. There were also two levels in the room, with a 'stage' area which the students could jump from, taking their lives (and my career) in their hands!

Unfortunately, it is a sad fact that many of us are 'stuck' with our problem rooms for a whole school year or for even longer. It is up to us, then, to find ways of minimizing the problems our space causes, so that our students are as comfortable and as well behaved as possible (and so that we are relaxed too!). How, then, can a teacher minimize the difficulty of working in a problem space?

Dealing with noise

Is the noise problem actually within the space (for instance, caused by a high ceiling), rather than coming from an external source? Is so, you need to think very carefully about how you might reduce the overall noise level of your lessons. In Chapter 3 – 'Control your voice' – we explored some strategies for doing this. Take care right from the start to keep your teaching voice low and controlled, and this will encourage your students to stay quiet to listen to you. Use the idea of a silence command but rather than using a whistle, which is a loud noise in itself, use a command such as raising your hand to get your students' attention.

In order to minimize the stress that constant high levels of noise can cause you as a teacher, you could divide your lessons into 'noisy' and 'quiet' times. For instance, you might follow a period of group work with a time for quiet reflection, perhaps watching groups of students present their ideas to the whole class, with the rest listening in silence. You might also take 'time outs' from noise, when the class must work in complete silence for five minutes or so, to give both you and them a break.

Dealing with temperature

There are in fact specified minimum and maximum temperatures for classrooms, and if you think that your own space might be contravening these rules, get hold of a thermometer and check! Teachers do have a tendency to suffer in silence, when in fact these regulations have been put in place to ensure their comfort and safety. Talk to your union representative or manager about dealing with the problem.

If you suffer from the sunlight heating up your classroom, then insist that blinds are fitted to your windows. In a hot space, students (and teachers) do tend to become ratty and bad-tempered more easily. Be aware of how the heat is affecting your temper, and try to stay calm and relaxed at all times. Make sure that you dress appropriately for your room, and tell your students to do so too. If your school has a rule about students taking their coats off, but your classroom is freezing, this could potentially lead to confrontations. Discuss this problem with a more senior member of staff – perhaps the rule could be relaxed if the room falls below a certain temperature level?

Dealing with lack of space

If your specific problem is a severe lack of space, look very carefully at the way you have laid out your classroom, and try several different options, preferably before your students arrive at the beginning of the school year. Why not try putting your desks in groups, rather than in rows, as this will generally take up less space in the room?

Think laterally too – perhaps it might help to turn the whole arrangement around, so that the desks are facing in an entirely different direction? If you do have to store resources in a small space, you could ask for some shelves to be put high up on the wall, so they don't take up any floor space.

11 The school

The school environment and behaviour

As we saw in Chapter 7, there are a range of reasons why students misbehave, and not all of them are directly related to the teacher. The school as a whole is a very specific type of environment, and one that can either encourage good behaviour or lead its students to see poor behaviour as acceptable. If you are in a school where behaviour is generally good, you may not be fully aware of all the factors that contribute to this. On the other hand, if you are in a school where behaviour tends to be bad, you might be blaming yourself and your teaching, whilst external factors are in fact at least partly to blame.

If you can develop an awareness of all the factors governing your students' behaviour, you are less likely to find yourself becoming stressed and defensive when your students do misbehave. Although there tends to be relatively little that individual teachers can do about the whole school environment and its impact on their own classroom teaching, we can certainly take some small steps both to minimize the effects, and also to change things for the better. What is it, then, about the school environment that can lead to bad behaviour? And what can we do to improve it?

The school buildings

As we saw in the previous chapter, our surroundings can have a huge impact on the way we feel and behave. If the school you work in is mostly run-down and dilapidated, with poor facilities, then it is possible that this could be having a negative effect on your students' behaviour as a whole, because their surroundings make them feel depressed. If the school population feel that no one cares about their school buildings, this may lead to an increased incidence of vandalism, and a general lack of care for the communal areas.

If you are in this situation, you could try to counteract the problems that it causes by making your classroom a real sanctuary for your children. Put up colourful and interesting displays, so that as soon as your students walk through your classroom door, they have a more positive frame of mind. In addition, why not organize a group or a class of students to help brighten up one area of the school? For instance, if you are a PE teacher, you might like to arrange a team of painters to add a mural to the changing rooms, or if you are a Science teacher, you could organize a group of children to take responsibility for creating and maintaining a nature area outside.

The whole-school ethos

The 'ethos' of a school is quite a difficult concept to pin down. It basically refers to the prevailing culture, the way that the students perceive the school, and their behaviour and work within it. If the ethos of your school is a positive one, this will have far-ranging implications for behaviour in your own classroom. If students arrive at the school and find an ethos of hard work and good behaviour, it is likely (unless they have severe or specific problems of their own) that they too will work hard and behave well. Unfortunately, once the ethos of a school becomes negative, it can take years of work to put things right. The culture of poor discipline filters down through all ages of students, so that the behaviour of those at the top of the school creates a climate of challenging authority right the way through. This in turn can become a self-perpetuating cycle that is very hard to break.

What, then, can you as an individual teacher do to help change the ethos of your own school? Again, if you can turn your own classroom into a place where the negative ethos cannot penetrate, then you will be contributing in a small but crucial way to the slow process of change. Teachers in a school with a negative ethos can tend to become cynical and demotivated, just like their students. Try to maintain a positive outlook, no matter how hard it is. If you find that there are not many extra curricular activities taking place in your school, why not organize a club to show your students how much you care about them, and about the school's progress as a whole?

Continuity of staff

'Good' schools will usually find it easy to attract and retain excellent teachers. The working conditions are good, the students want to learn, and the teachers will enjoy their jobs so much that they don't actually want to leave. Unfortunately for 'bad' schools, this situation is reversed. It is hard for these schools to recruit and retain well-motivated teachers, and the constant turnover of staff leads to a negative attitude in the students. They start to feel that the teachers don't really care for them because they keep leaving them. There is a lack of continuity in the teaching, especially if staff leave midway through the school year. It is very hard for the teachers and students to develop positive relationships with each other, and the teaching staff can soon lose their motivation. This lack of continuity becomes a self-perpetuating downward spiral that is hard for a school to break out of.

In reality, the best way for you to contribute to the continuity of staff within your own school is by staying there for a long time. In addition, you could support and mentor newer teachers, encouraging them to see the long-term picture, and creating a positive attitude amongst the staff. Obviously, it is up to you to decide whether you are willing to put up with the conditions in which you find yourself.

The management of the school

The way a school is managed can have a significant impact on the behaviour you find within your classroom. If the students see a strong leadership team, who focus keenly on supporting and developing the staff of the school, and who value their teachers highly, then they are likely to have a greater sense of respect for you as their class teacher. As well as this, you will know that you have managers to turn to if you are having problems, and this will give you a greater sense of security.

The management of a school is generally divided into a senior leadership team, including the head teacher, and one or more deputy heads. Below this is the curriculum management team, perhaps key stage or core subject leaders in a primary school, or heads of department or faculty in a secondary school. A supportive manager or head of department can be a huge bonus to a teacher who is struggling with control in their classroom. Your students should see a clear link between the normal teachers and the managers at your school. In the ideal situation, teachers should be able to refer their most difficult students to a 'higher power' who can take the problem one stage further. Do talk regularly to your managers, asking them for advice or help in class if you need it.

Whole-school behaviour policies

If it is effective and well thought out, your whole-school behaviour policy will be an invaluable aid in helping you control behaviour in your classroom. Different types of school have very different and specific behavioural problems, and ideally the whole-school behaviour policy should be linked closely to the particular difficulties your school faces. A good whole-school behaviour policy will offer the teacher a number of sanction levels to work with when disciplining their students, and also a way of 'keeping tabs' on the overall behaviour of each individual within the school.

Teachers at the chalkface have a very strong idea of what's going wrong (or right!) on a whole-school basis. They will often chat about behaviour problems in the staffroom, and in my experience teachers tend to raise very similar concerns over whole-school behaviour issues. An effective management team will listen carefully to what their teachers say and develop their whole-school behaviour policy in conjunction with their staff. A good whole-school behaviour policy will be in a constant state of change. Such a policy needs to keep developing, not only to improve, but also because the staff and children are constantly changing as well.

In addition to constantly evolving, for a whole-school policy to be fully effective, it will need to be consistently applied, so that the students know exactly what to expect from a teacher if they do misbehave. There should be a very clear set of rules, and a very clear pattern of sanctions that will happen if students choose to break them. This consistency is a vital part of making a whole-school behaviour policy effective, and it is perhaps one of the hardest things to achieve, simply because teachers are all individuals who will apply the policy in their own different ways. If a school can achieve a consistent application of the policy, the students will respond much better, as they see that the boundaries set for them are fixed and invariable – they cannot get away with behaviour 'X', whoever the teacher!

Let's take a brief look now at some of the different components of a typical whole-school behaviour policy, to see how and why they might be effective. If you do feel that your school behaviour policy is not working particularly well, you might like to suggest including some of the following ideas to help improve it. You will usually have the opportunity to do this through the meetings structure in your school.

The 'school rules'

When creating a whole-school behaviour policy, the school will need to decide exactly what types of behaviour are acceptable and unacceptable. This will probably result in a list of rules, whereby the students (and their parents) know exactly what is expected. These rules might refer to how they should work, to behaviour in the classroom and around the school building, and may also include details about what uniform is required, and how the students should treat each other, their teachers, and the environment as a whole. Many schools will provide each teacher or classroom with a laminated set of these rules, so that you can refer to them as you sanction. If your school does not give you a printed set of rules, do make one of your own to go on your classroom wall.

A set of rules will make any teacher's life easier, as they can then refer to these when they are giving a punishment, making it clear that they are simply following the school policy, rather than personally 'attacking' the student. Some schools do choose to make life difficult for their staff, by setting rules that will inevitably lead to confrontations. Some of the rules that teachers are asked to apply can seem remarkably petty, both to the teacher and to the students. When a teacher is put in this situation, it is clearly up to the individual how keenly they apply that particular rule. Unfortunately, once we start picking and choosing about which rules we employ, the consistency of the whole-school behaviour policy is damaged. It is far better, surely, for schools to ensure that their rules are sensible in the first place, by consulting closely with their staff (and with their students).

Sanctions

Most schools operate a system of sanctions where the punishments build up gradually, but always in the same format. The initial sanction might be a verbal warning, followed by a written warning, and then building up to detentions of increasing length. There might also be an added punishment for students who get to the highest level of sanction, for instance the teacher making a phone call home.

A gradual and invariable build-up of sanctions offers the teacher a good way of maintaining control, because they have a set pattern to follow in every instance. The steady build-up will also help avoid confrontation, because there are plenty of chances for the student to co-operate by behaving properly, rather than receiving a more severe punishment. Again, it is important that these levels are used consistently across the school, or the students may view certain teachers as unfair.

The 'ultimate' sanction

Most schools now offer their teachers an 'ultimate' sanction, whereby a situation that has gone out of control can be retrieved, usually by removing the student from the classroom. It could be that a student is becoming physically violent, or simply that their behaviour is so unacceptable that the teacher cannot continue their lesson if the student remains in the room. In this type of situation, there would normally be a senior teacher available to go to the classroom and remove the student. The class teacher might send for help, perhaps by the use of a 'red card' or a special slip, that one of their students takes to the office to summon the senior teacher.

It is perhaps a sad reflection of the situation in some of our classrooms that such a severe sanction could be necessary. In reality the ultimate sanction offers a much-needed 'fall back' position for when behaviour becomes completely unacceptable or even danger-ous to the teacher and to the rest of the class. For this sanction to work properly, the teacher must not feel scared about using it. There should be no sense that the teacher has failed if they need to apply this sanction.

The points system

Much of the misbehaviour that teachers face on a daily basis is, thankfully, small-scale disruption, rather than the serious types of incident described above. However, schools do need to develop some way of dealing with these small-scale incidents, which can interrupt learning in the classroom if they are not dealt with properly. There are many students who repeat a certain type of low-level misdemeanour over and over again, and an effective school behaviour policy needs to find a way of dealing with this problem.

One idea that I have seen used to great effect is a 'points system'. For each type of misdemeanour, the student earns a certain number of points, ranging from one or two points for a small disruption or infraction, to a higher number of points for serious incidents. Points can also be given for breaking the school rules, for instance if a student is not in correct school uniform, or is late to school. The total level of points that a student has earned then allows the school to see exactly who it is that is refusing to comply with the school code.

Support systems

When we are having problems controlling behaviour, what we most need are good support systems, someone that we trust enough to share our worries with, or someone who can give us specialist advice on a particular issue. By its very nature, teaching is a solitary occupation, and alone in your classroom, you have very little idea about what is going on elsewhere in your school. It is all too easy for the imagination to run riot, and to find yourself thinking that all the other teachers in your school have perfect behaviour in *their* classrooms: to imagine that it is only you who *cannot* get the buggers to behave. Poor behaviour can make you feel depressed and alone, but with an effective support system in place, you will always have someone to turn to when you are feeling down.

Other teachers
Teachers tend to develop very strong relationships with their colleagues, perhaps because the work that they do can be so physically and emotionally taxing, and they therefore share a common bond with each other. Although in reality you spend little time during your working day with other teachers at your school, you may well find yourself socializing with them outside work. Do take the time to go to the staffroom during the day. This will give you a chance to refresh yourself – a tired teacher is far more likely to deal with poor behaviour in a negative way. It will also give

you an opportunity to chat with other teachers about any problems you have experienced that day.

Special needs staff

As I have mentioned before, the special needs staff at your school can be an invaluable resource for you when dealing with behaviour in your classroom. Not only do they have specialist knowledge of the problems you are experiencing, they will also be aware of exactly how bad behaviour can make you feel. Get to know these staff, ask their advice and get as much information from them as you can about how to handle your problem children.

Managers

Depending on how well you relate to them, your managers can also be a helpful source of comfort and inspiration. Teachers in a management position will generally have at least a few years' experience, and if you are a relatively inexperienced teacher, they will be able to advise you because they will have encountered many of the problems you are currently facing. In addition, your direct manager should be able to take on some responsibility for ensuring that your students behave. If you are having difficulty with a particular individual, it may be that you need to refer the situation to a higher authority such as a curriculum leader or a deputy head.

The unions

Your union representative can also be an excellent support, particularly if you are facing severe behaviour problems. As we have noted, there may be health and safety concerns in your classroom (both with the room itself and with the students inside it) that your union representative can advise you about. If you are put in a position where a student makes a complaint about you (an increasing problem nowadays, it seems) then your union representative will advise you on legal issues and other questions relating to your career.

Age-specific strategies

Although the advice given in this book applies to students of all different ages, there are certain strategies that are more suited to controlling the behaviour of children at specific stages in their school life. As they become more experienced, teachers very quickly learn what techniques suit students of different ages. You might find, however, that you have been working with Reception-level children for a couple of years, and you are then asked to switch to teaching a class of Year 3 students.

The age-specific strategies that I give below are based on three times in a child's schooling: the very young, in Nursery or Reception; the mid point, at about Year 6 or Year 7; and the last years of statutory schooling, when students are doing their GCSE courses, in Years 10 and 11.

Young children (4–6 years)

As we saw in Chapter 7 ('How students change'), young children can find school a very confusing and frightening place. Teachers do need to take this into account when dealing with poor behaviour. At this stage, a pattern for the rest of their school careers is being set, and clearly we want to create a positive model of good behaviour. Ideally, we need to avoid scaring young children into behaving well, and rather try to encourage them by using more positive means. Here are a few ideas specifically about working with young children:

- *Make your instructions very clear:* Young children can find it hard to 'take in' all the things that are going on around them. After all, only recently their parents or guardians were their whole world. Now they are at school, where many different things are going on, and they can be easily distracted (see below). When you are giving instructions to young children, you need to do so with a clear voice, using simple words and a relatively slow tone. Repetition is also vital for ensuring that young children understand what we have asked them. A useful idea is to ask your students to repeat the instructions you have given them, and you can then clarify any misunderstandings or confusions.
- *Train them now!:* In the film *Kindergarten Cop*, Arnold Schwarzenegger trains his class of young children as though they were at 'police academy'. Whilst this fictional example might seem a little extreme, it does in fact demonstrate a very effective point about working with young children. If

you can train them to behave well right at the beginning, they will (usually) happily follow your instructions from then onwards. For instance, you could have a set of drawers where your children keep their things. On a signal from you, they could be trained to go to the drawers a few at a time, collect their work things, and then come back to sit on the carpet.

- *Make behaving well fun!:* As an extension of the idea above, you should always aim to make good behaviour seem like fun. If you can achieve this, your children will be only too happy to behave well. For example, you can turn pretty much anything into a 'game' with young children. For instance, the game 'sleeping lions', where the children lie down as still as possible and pretend to sleep, can be a very effective way of calming your class down for a story at the end of the day.

- *Use control signals:* Control signals can be very helpful when you are working with young children. They may become totally engrossed in an activity, perhaps making quite a lot of noise. You need to find a way to gain their attention quickly and effectively. One idea that I have used to good effect is to start clapping in a particular pattern. The children must then join in until the whole class is clapping the pattern. You can then slow down gradually, and when you stop clapping there could be a rule that they come to sit down on the carpet.

- *Distract them from poor behaviour:* The younger we are, the more easily we can be distracted from a certain course of action. If you do find incidents of misbehaviour are cropping up, try to use a distraction as a way of nipping the incident in the bud. For example, if little Annie is having a temper tantrum, you could bring out a finger puppet who talks to her in a silly voice to distract her.

- *Use a 'teacher-y' tone:* The way that you address young children can have a big impact on their behaviour. In my experience, I have found that using a slightly exaggerated 'teacher-y' tone can be most effective. While you should always avoid patronizing young children (or anyone, for that matter!), this tone of voice is calm, clear, fairly slow, but very well modulated (i.e. moving between tones, such as happy, surprised, and so on).

The mid point (10–12 years)

At this stage in their lives, your students are preparing to make the transition from child to young adult. They are on the cusp of becoming a teenager, but are not yet quite ready to shrug off some of the childish feelings and emotions that may lead to immature and silly behaviour. As we have seen, in the top year at their primary or middle school, your students may be confident as a result of being 'top dogs'. Things change dramatically when they arrive at secondary school, where they are once again at the bottom of the pile. At this age, children may look up to those older than them for an example of how to behave. They could also start to push at the boundaries and test adult authority, as they take the first step on the road to becoming a grown-up. Here are a few ideas for age-specific strategies taken from my experience of teaching students in Year 7:

- *Take them seriously:* At this age, children often view themselves as more grown up than they actually are. If we want them to behave in a mature fashion, then we must take their feelings seriously. Avoid at all costs talking down to students at this stage of their school lives. If you patronize them, they will react badly. If you treat them as young adults, they will often live up to your expectations and surprise you with the adult way that they act and behave.
- *Offer a positive role model:* Children of this age need good role models to look up to and learn from. Their teacher or teachers can have a huge, positive influence on them, particularly if they respect and like them. Other, older students can also offer constructive or harmful examples. If you teach a Year 6 class, they will probably be nervous and uncertain about the transition to secondary school. Why not bring in a secondary school student to offer them a positive example and to talk to them about what the move will entail?
- *Know what interests them:* This is a time when children start to take a keen interest in the wider world, and in the cultural icons that surround them in the media. They are starting to

gain their independence, and their parents may be giving them more freedom to buy their own clothes and music, or to stay out later in the evenings. Find out what interests your class – the latest boy band, or the famous football player – and try to incorporate these interests into your teaching, or at least chat to your students about them to show that you too are up to date on the latest cultural developments. As we have seen, if you can personalize your teaching in this way, you are likely to encourage better behaviour.

- *Understand their fears and concerns:* When they first start at secondary school, children may be fearful of looking odd to their peers, or they may feel embarrassed about their relationship with the opposite gender. Do try to think back to how you felt at this age – if you ask your students to work boy/girl, do not be surprised if they react negatively. They are probably trying to cover up their embarrassment!

GCSE level (14–16 years)

This can be a very exciting age group to teach, but it can also be one of the most challenging, if behaviour is a problem. Students between 14 and 16 years old are practically grown up, and in our modern world they have many adult concerns that are nothing to do with education! There is a great deal of pressure on students as they lead up to their GCSE exams. They may also be considering leaving education, moving outside the safe, enclosed environment of a school and into the real world. Here are a few thoughts about handling the behaviour of students in this age group:

- *Treat them as adults:* To all intents and purposes, students of this age are effectively adults, especially those who are 16. If you want respect and good behaviour from them, you will need to talk to them and work with them on an adult level. There really is little point in being a 'strict and scary' teacher at this stage. These young adults will generally react badly to this confrontational style, and may feel that you are patronizing them. In the work place it would be expected that superiors would communicate to staff in a civil manner to discuss a problem; why should things be any different at school?

- *Be willing to stretch the boundaries:* Some of the rules and boundaries that are set in a school can seem pretty meaningless to students of this age. After all, why shouldn't they wear a coat if they are cold, or chew gum if they wish? Your priority at this stage must be their learning, and you should avoid the application of petty rules if at all possible, especially if these are likely to lead to serious friction. Similarly, these young adults see swearing all around them – on the television, in their social life, from their families and friends. Ignoring the odd swear word will make you seem more human, and will also help you avoid pointless conflict with your classes.
- *Make them take responsibility:* Once out in the world, and working in a job, your students will need to behave properly, or they will be sacked! At this stage of their school lives, they must take responsibility for their behaviour and for their learning. Point this out to them when they do misbehave. If you treat them like adults, they must learn to take an adult level of responsibility for their behaviour. Expect the best from them and hopefully you won't be disappointed!
- *Understand their concerns:* At this age, your students may have some serious concerns that are unconnected to their schooling. They may be having boyfriend or girlfriend problems that affect the way they behave in your lessons. Do try to understand this – just as you have worries outside of school, so do they. If you are a particularly sympathetic teacher, you may find that some of your students approach you to talk about a personal problem. Do make sure that you take the time to discuss their problem on an adult level with them. Ensure too that you refer the difficulty to the relevant member of staff at your school if it seems necessary, particularly if it is a child welfare issue, such as a teenage pregnancy.

Handling the transition

The transition from middle to secondary school can be an extremely difficult time for our students. In Year 6, they will be full of concerns about what secondary school might actually be like, and once they reach Year 7, they may find the new environment confusing and threatening. If we can minimize the trauma that the transition causes, then we can hope to also reduce the negative effects on behaviour that may result. But how can we achieve this?

Many schools now have a teacher whose responsibility it is to oversee the transition to secondary school. This teacher might go to visit students in Year 6, to talk to them about their concerns and answer any questions that they might have. They could also organize visits for the Year 6 students to the secondary school, so that they can spend a day looking around, and talking to some of the students who are already there. Often, the new Year 7 students will start at secondary school a day or more before the rest of the school returns from holidays. This gives them some time to settle in before the mass of students arrive.

Another useful idea that I have seen used is letters written in English lessons from current Year 7s to the Year 6s below them. In these letters they can tell them all about the 'truth' of secondary school, and dispel many of those rumours which amazingly still float around, such as having your head flushed down the toilet! Having a 'contact' at secondary school can also lessen the fear when they do start there – at least the Year 6s will know one person when they arrive!

Part Five

For Example ...

12 'Minor' behaviour problems

The examples

In this chapter and the next we will be looking at some examples of a teacher dealing with behaviour problems. By reading these examples you will see how the ideas in this book actually work in practice. The examples deal with various different incidents of misbehaviour and are set at a variety of ages across the primary and secondary sectors, although they are easily applicable to any age group. For each incident, two examples are given to show how you might handle the problem in a 'good' or a 'bad' way. The examples are written as play scripts with some general information about the situation, then a chance to see how the teacher deals with it. At the end of each example a commentary is given, discussing what the teacher did, what strategies he or she used (or failed to use!), and exactly how these tactics worked. You might like to act out some of these scripts on a training day for a hands-on experience of the different methods shown!

We will be dealing with the 'minor' behaviour problems, low-level disruptions such as a talkative class or a student who is chewing gum. These are the sort of problems which can usually be dealt with relatively easily. If you can solve these minor difficulties in a calm and consistent way, you should be able to encourage better behaviour from all your students. In addition, it is likely that you will avoid serious confrontations in your classroom, because the students will see that they cannot get away with anything, no matter how minor! On the other hand, if you deal with these problems badly, you might exacerbate the situation so that more serious incidents do occur. Just take a look at the 'bad' examples to see what can happen when things get out of hand!

The talkative class

Age group: Year 7.
Details of the problem: Although this class is generally good natured and well behaved, they can be incredibly talkative. This is causing Miss Flynn problems, particularly at the start of the lesson when she wants to settle them down, take the register, and get on with the work.

A good example

The class arrives for the lesson, chatting away happily. Miss Flynn is standing at the door, blocking the entrance, arms folded, looking mean.

Miss Flynn: Right! Today we're going to line up before we come in the room. I want to see how quickly you can line up in silence. Five ... four ... three ... two ... one ...

The class is now lined up, but the students are still chatting amongst themselves. Miss Flynn coughs and looks at her watch, but doesn't say anything. She waits a moment to see whether they will become silent without any intervention, but they continue talking.

Miss Flynn: *[Apparently talking to herself.]* Oh dear. They're not silent. And that's what I wanted before I let them in the room, because I needed to talk to them. Oh well, it looks like they're going to be spending some of their break time with me. What a shame. And they're such a nice class, although they are just too chatty. *[She sighs and looks at her watch.]* That's one minute wasted, so that's one minute at break time.

The class realizes what is going on, and the more observant students 'shush' the others. There is still some low-level chatter, though.

Miss Flynn: *[Looking at her watch again.]* Well, some of them are listening, but that's still two minutes wasted. Of course, I might allow them to win the time back if they can all be silent in five ... four ... three ... two ... one ... zero!

It works! Miss Flynn can now address the class and let them in the room.

Miss Flynn: That's excellent. Well done. Now, that is how we are going to start every lesson from this point onwards – lined up in silence, waiting outside the classroom. I've decided that you're becoming rather too talkative and I'm going to stamp it out. Right. I want you to come into the classroom quietly and sensibly. As soon as you are in your seats, I want you to get your books and pens out, and sit in silence, so that I can take the register. The first person ready, sitting in silence, gets a merit!

The class hurries inside, and by the time Miss Flynn comes in, they are all waiting in silence!

Commentary on the good example

The teacher has decided to use a fairly light approach to deal with the problem, although with a touch of strictness as necessary. This kind of style is well suited to Year 7 students – if the teacher suddenly needs to clamp down on them, she could simply raise her voice slightly, or change her tone. When the students arrive, she is ready and waiting for them, her strategy already planned. The first thing she does is set the class a challenge, with a time limit, counting down from five to see whether this will work. It does to a certain extent, because the students are now in a straight line (useful because she can see all their faces). Unfortunately they are still chatting.

Now the teacher decides to use a rather unusual technique. She acts as though she is talking to herself, telling herself what she wanted from the class, how they are failing to meet her expectations, how she does in fact really like them, and finally what the result of their continued chatter will be. By appearing to talk to herself, she is in fact thinking out loud, completely depersonalizing the sanction she gives. The students start to respond and, capitalizing on this, the teacher offers them a get-out clause of winning back the detention time. Finally, she again uses the countdown technique and this time it works!

Once the class is completely silent and attentive, the teacher can talk to them about why she wants them to line up in this way. She sets the standard for the future, so that they know what is expected of them when they come to her lesson next time. Lastly, she gives them a target to achieve, with a reward for the first to manage it

(Year 7 generally love to compete!) – to get into the room quickly and quietly and let her take the register in silence. Notice how, throughout the encounter, the teacher remains relentlessly polite and calm.

A Bad Example

The class arrives for the lesson, chatting away happily. Miss Flynn is inside the classroom, doing some last-minute preparation. When she sees them starting to come in, she waves them back outside.

Miss Flynn: No, no, no! Get out! Out! I'm not letting you lot in here until you're quiet. Get back outside and wait for me.

James, a nice, quiet, well-behaved student is already sitting at his desk, getting his pencil case and books out.

Miss Flynn: James! Out I said! I can't believe it! What is wrong with you today? You're normally so nice. Pack your stuff up and get out!

James: But miss . . .

Miss Flynn: Don't you 'but miss' me, young man. Just shut up and do what I say.

More students are arriving, and Miss Flynn backs them up to the door, waving her hands at them.

Miss Flynn: Outside. Outside, I said! I want you lot lined up and silent.

The class makes a vague sort of line, but there is still quite a lot of talking.

Miss Flynn: Right, shut up you lot, I want to talk to you.

James is talking to the student behind him, telling her to be quiet for Miss Flynn.

Miss Flynn: James! Didn't you hear me? I said be quiet. That's the second time you've disobeyed me today. Right. You're in detention with me after the lesson.

James: But Miss . . . that's not fair! I was only telling . . .

Miss Flynn: Don't talk back to me. You were talking, now you're in detention. Now can you lot please shut up and let me get on with it.

By now the students are either engrossed in watching the confrontation between Miss Flynn and James, or are chatting amongst themselves because they are bored with waiting.

Miss Flynn: *[Starting to lose her temper.]* I said be quiet! SHUT UP!!!

The class quietens down, although a few of the more regular trouble-makers are at the back, still talking.

Miss Flynn: Right, when you get inside sit down and be silent so I can take the register. Okay? Come on then, in you come.

Commentary on the bad example

Right from the start of the lesson, it is clear that Miss Flynn is not well prepared for this encounter. If she does want to change her usual routine, this must be planned in advance, and she must be ready to interact with the class immediately they arrive. From the word go, when she flaps at them to leave her room, she is setting the seeds for a negative lesson. In fact, her very first word is *'No'*! When they start to come into the room (as they are used to doing) she acts as though they are trespassing on her space. This inconsistency is bound to set up at least minor confrontations.

Her next mistake is to pick on poor James – a well-behaved student who is simply doing what he normally does, getting ready for the lesson! She immediately asks him what is 'wrong with him', a very negative comment, compounded with rudeness when she tells him to 'shut up'. Once the teacher has waved the students outside, there is already a feeling of disquiet about this lesson, and it is not surprising that they do not follow her instructions. Again, she is rude, telling them to shut up. She then picks on James unfairly – he is trying to get one of the other students to be quiet, but she accuses him of disobeying her and gives him an unearned sanction. If James was a confrontational type of student, this could have led to a more serious incident.

The class is now confused and bored – they had arrived at the lesson expecting consistency, and things are not turning out as normal. Because they are not fulfilling her (unrealistic) expectations, the teacher loses her temper. This does quieten the class down, but she then allows the students inside without having their full attention. At this stage, it seems to have been totally pointless for her to insist that they go outside and line up – she has achieved nothing! The 'troublemakers' at the back of the line have got away with their misbehaviour, and the lining-up activity is therefore pretty meaningless. At this point, it is likely that the class will take a long time to settle once inside the room, and they will have a negative view of the whole encounter.

Chewing gum

Age group: Year 9.
Details of the problem: Chewing gum is not allowed in the school. A few members of the class are consistently ignoring this rule. The same students are also proving to be amongst the more disruptive element of the group.

A good example
The class is working on an individual task. Mr Everall is going around the room, helping them. He notices that Sundip is chewing. He goes to the front of the classroom, picks up the bin, and holds it under Sundip's mouth.

Mr Everall: Sundip! Gum in the bin. Now. You know the rule.
   Sundip: But sir! I'm not chewing.
Mr Everall: Yes you are. Spit it out. NOW.
   Sundip: I've swallowed it, sir. Look. *[He opens his mouth wide.]*
Mr Everall: I'll take your word on that, Sundip. But if I catch you chewing again this lesson, you're in big trouble.

Later on in the lesson, Mr Everall notices that Sundip is chewing again.

Mr Everall: Sundip. Could you come over here please. *[He walks over to the bin.]*
   Sundip: What sir?
Mr Everall: Over here please.

Sundip comes over to where the teacher is standing.

Mr Everall: See that?
   Sundip: What?

Mr Everall: The bin.
    Sundip: What about it?

Leaning towards Sundip and speaking quietly in his ear so that none of the class can hear.

Mr Everall: Put the gum in there NOW. And don't give me 'I'm
    not chewing', because I saw you. You can stay behind
    for five minutes after the lesson to clean up my room.
    Any more rubbish from you, and you'll be in a half-
    hour detention.

Sundip spits out the gum and sheepishly goes to sit back down.

Commentary on the good example
This Year 9 class requires a slightly different, harder approach than
the Year 7s in the previous incident. Because there is a disruptive
element in the group, it is essential that the teacher makes his
control of the situation very clear. His first approach is to demand in
front of the whole class that the student puts the gum in the bin: the
class already knows the rule about no gum and this student is plainly
disobeying. Although this might seem quite a minor problem, if the
teacher clamps down on it now, his overall authority will be
reinforced because he has shown himself willing to apply all the
school rules.

As often happens, the student claims to have already swallowed
the gum, thus making the teacher's demand void. Instead of getting
into a big scene about this, the teacher warns the student what will
happen if he is caught again. Later on in the lesson, the same
situation arises. This time, the teacher takes a different approach,
dealing with it in a more private way. He gets the student to come
to him (always a useful way of showing your high status) and then
demands that he puts the gum into the bin, making it perfectly clear
that this time the student must not 'try it on'. He then sanctions the
student as promised, making the punishment fit the crime, and
warning him that any further disobedience will result in a longer
penalty.

A bad example

The class is working on an individual task. Mr Everall is going around the room, helping them. He notices that Sundip is chewing.

Mr Everall: Sundip? Are you chewing?

Sundip: No sir.

Mr Everall: Yes you are. I saw you.

Sundip: No I'm not, sir. Look. *[He opens his mouth wide.]*

Mr Everall: I saw you chewing. Don't give me that rubbish. Could you go and spit the gum in the bin please?

Sundip: But, sir. I'm not chewing.

Mr Everall: You'd better not be.

Later on in the lesson, Mr Everall notices that Sundip is chewing again.

Mr Everall: Sundip. I thought you said you weren't chewing?

Sundip: I'm not. I'm just biting the inside of my mouth. I do that when I'm bored.

Mr Everall: Are you sure?

Sundip: Absolutely sure.

Mr Everall: Okay then.

Commentary on the bad example

This example is 'bad', not because a confrontation occurs, but because the student ends up 'getting one over' on the teacher. In a class where there are troublemakers, this can be a dangerous precedent, because if a student gets away with minor misbehaviour like this, he or she starts to push the boundaries to see exactly how far they can go before being sanctioned. It is your decision as a teacher whether or not you apply rules such as the banning of chewing gum. You need to ask yourself – is it worth the confrontations that might occur? And can you use the rule to demonstrate your control over the class in a calm and consistent way?

The teacher's style here is very defensive (see Chapter 4 – 'Attack and defence'). He asks the student whether he is chewing, rather than stating that he has seen him doing so. He also avoids sanctioning the student, perhaps because he is nervous about what might happen if he does. In this example, the student clearly wins the encounter – all the 'certain' statements are made by the student, rather than by the teacher.

The plasticine flicker

Age group: Year 2.

Details of the problem: Sally is a real handful. She is very lively, and if she gets bored in lessons she starts to flick plasticine at the other students. The teacher rarely sees her doing this, but the other children in the class keep complaining, and at the end of the school day, Miss Burn's carpet is always covered in little bits of plasticine!

A good example

The class is working in small groups on a weighing activity. They are weighing different substances to see which ones are heavy and which ones are light. Unfortunately, one of the things that they have to weigh is plasticine! Miss Burn is keeping a close eye on Sally's group. She notices that they are about to weigh the plasticine.

Miss Burn: Well done, red group. You've managed to weigh all these different things so far. What did you find out about them?

Ben: The tissue paper is really light, miss.

Miss Burn: That's great, Ben. What else did you find out?

Robert: The metal block was very heavy.

Miss Burn: Excellent, Robert. What about the plasticine? Sally. Do you think that's going to be heavy or light?

Sally: Light, miss.

Miss Burn: Are you sure, Sally? Shall we try it now?

Sally: Okay. *[She weighs it.]* Oh. It's heavy, miss.

Miss Burn: And when something is heavy, what could happen if we throw it at someone? Ben. What do you think?

Ben: You might hurt them, miss?

Miss Burn: That's right. Now, Sally. Do you think it's a good idea to throw a metal block at someone?

Sally: Definitely not, miss.

Miss Burn: And plasticine?

Sally: Well, you could just throw a little bit. Then it wouldn't hurt them.

Miss Burn: But what if it got in their eyes?

Robert: That would hurt loads! I got some soap in my eyes and it really hurt. Plasticine might be like that.

Miss Burn: And what could happen if we got plasticine on the carpet?

Robert: It could go all sticky. Look, miss, there's some on the carpet here. Uggh!

Miss Burn: Do you think it's ever right to throw things, Ben?

Ben: Well ... you can throw a ball in the playground, miss.

Miss Burn: But what about in the classroom? What do you think, Sally?

Sally: No. We shouldn't throw things at all miss.

Commentary on the good example

In this example, the teacher comes at the problem from a lateral direction. Rather than catching Sally in the act of throwing (which she would have had problems doing), she decides to approach the issue by discussing it, trying to make the children understand *why* they shouldn't throw things. She approaches the group just as they are about to tackle the plasticine, and immediately praises them for the way they are working, setting up a positive feeling about the whole encounter.

She discusses the activity with them, making sure they all contribute, and leading up to the issue of why it might be dangerous to throw plasticine. At no point does she actually accuse Sally of throwing plasticine, but what she does do is point out the problems that might be caused if anyone happened to do this. The whole issue is completely depersonalized, and the student will hopefully be forced to reconsider his/her behaviour. If she does continue to flick plasticine, the teacher can simply refer back to this discussion, making clear the reasons for stopping the behaviour.

A bad example

The class is working in small groups on an art activity. They are making plasticine models of farm animals for a project. Miss Burn is helping green group when she gets hit on the head by a plasticine pellet.

Miss Burn: Ow! Who threw that? That really hurt me. Sally? Was it you? I've seen you throwing plasticine before.

Sally: No miss. It wasn't me. It was Josh.

Josh: No it wasn't. It was you, Sally, I saw you.

Miss Burn: Sally. Not only do you throw plasticine at me, but you're also a liar. That's very naughty.

Sally: I didn't throw it. Josh is lying.

Josh: No I'm not. You're the liar. Liar! Liar!

Miss Burn: Stop it! Both of you! Go and sit on the carpet. If you can't behave yourselves, then no fun activities for you.

Sally and Josh go to sit on the carpet. A few minutes later a fight starts between them.

Miss Burn: STOP THAT RIGHT NOW!

Commentary on the bad example

This encounter seems doomed to failure right from the start. Because the teacher has actually been hit by the pellet, she is emotional about the situation, rather than approaching it in a calm, quiet way. Her immediate reaction is to accuse Sally. Although she may well be correct in doing so, it does seem unfair to blame the student without any proof. Sally, probably embarrassed about her behaviour, tries to lay the blame on another student. Josh understandably feels aggrieved about this. In the end, he is sanctioned when he has done nothing wrong. The incident ends with the children being punished, but the punishment deprives them of the chance to do their work. Far better to sanction them in a way that does not impact on their learning, but instead makes them address their behaviour.

It is hardly surprising that a fight starts between the two children when they are sitting on the carpet, bored, with nothing to do. They are watching the others do a fun activity, and for Josh particularly this must seem very unfair – all he did was defend himself when he was falsely accused!

13 'Major' behaviour problems

The examples

In this chapter we will be dealing with the more serious behaviour problems that occur in the classroom. These incidents can make a teacher feel extremely threatened, and after they take place, can leave you in a vulnerable and unhappy state. Happily, in the majority of schools these events are still relatively rare. By looking at ways of dealing with these serious incidents *before* they occur, I hope to arm you with the knowledge that you will need if you do face such an event in your classroom.

When dealing with a serious confrontation, one of the most essential things is to ensure your own safety, and that of the students in your class. If a situation seems likely to blow up, never be afraid to use the 'ultimate sanction' (see Chapters 5 and 11). There is no shame at all in using such a sanction – it is there for just these circumstances. And I hope, by following the advice given in this book, and in this chapter, you will be able to stop these conflicts developing in the first place.

Let's take a look now at some examples that show you how to deal with major incidents of misbehaviour. Just as in the last chapter, we will see a good and a bad example of each event, with a commentary to follow that explains how and why the strategies used work or don't work. Because I want these examples to be as realistic as possible, I have included the swearing that, in my experience, often accompanies serious incidents. I have, of course, replaced the swear words with asterisks – I leave it up to your imagination to fill in the blanks!

The threat of physical aggression

Age group: Year 10.
Details of the problem: Colin is a very difficult student, whose temper flares easily and often. During a lesson, he becomes involved in an argument with Patrick which quickly threatens to turn into a physical fight.

A good example

Colin and Patrick are arguing about who owns a CD. Colin claims that he lent it to Patrick, but Patrick disagrees.

Colin: Give it back, you ✻✻✻✻✻✻!
Patrick: Get real, Colin. It's mine. I never lent it to you.
Miss Cook: Colin. Patrick. I want you both to calm down please.
Colin: He nicked my CD, miss.
Patrick: He called me a ✻✻✻✻✻✻, miss!
Miss Cook: Look, I want you both to get on with your work. And I want you to stop using foul language before I have to punish you for it. Give me the CD, Patrick, and we'll sort this out at the end of the lesson.
Patrick: No way. It's my CD.
Miss Cook: Patrick. Give me the CD *NOW*. No arguing. And go and sit over there away from Colin please. *[She points to the far side of the classroom.]*

He hands it over grudgingly and moves to sit across the room. The boys settle to work, but a few minutes later they start arguing again across the classroom.

Colin: I'm gonna get you after school, you ✻✻✻✻.
Patrick: Oh yeah? Well I'm gonna mash your head you stupid ✻✻✻✻✻✻!
Miss Cook: Right, that's enough. Colin, Patrick. Outside *NOW*.
Patrick: I'm not going outside. I ain't done nothin'.
Miss Cook: Both of you outside *NOW*. I mean it. Don't mess with me.

The boys and Miss Cook go outside the room. She stands between them so that they can't get to each other.

Miss Cook: Right. We're going to sort this out now. I have the CD, and if there's any more rubbish about fighting from either of you, I'm going to give it to the Head. Then he can decide whether or not you get it back. Patrick? What do you say? Are you going to get on with your work? No more nonsense?

Patrick: Alright, miss.

Miss Cook: Good. Very sensible. Right. You go inside. I want to talk to Colin on his own. *[Patrick goes back in.]*

Colin: I'm gonna punch him, miss. I don't care what you say.

Miss Cook: Colin. You are making me extremely unhappy with this attitude. If you punch Patrick, you'll get yourself into trouble. You'll probably be excluded again. Is that what you really want?

Colin: No.

Miss Cook: I want us to sort this out by talking about it. Tell me about the CD.

Colin: My sister bought it for me. I lent it to Patrick, but he won't give it back. He's a ****.

Miss Cook: Colin, I'm going to pretend I didn't hear that. But if you swear again, we'll go straight to the head of department and she can sort this out.

Colin: Sorry miss.

Miss Cook: Right. Your sister's in year 9, isn't she? Could we find her at break and check with her? If she agrees with what you say, then you can have the CD back.

Colin: Okay.

Miss Cook: Right, Colin. Now I want you to sit out here to work for the rest of the lesson.

Colin: Why? That's not fair.

Miss Cook: Do you want to get into a fight with Patrick? No? Well, I'm saving you the temptation if you sit outside. We'll sort out your CD at break, okay?

Colin agrees. Miss Cook brings him out a desk and chair to work at.

Commentary on the good example

The teacher intervenes quickly as the argument starts, hoping to stop it before it develops. Such early intervention can often prevent a minor confrontation spiralling out of control (see Chapter 3). She chooses not to punish the bad language that Colin has used, because she knows that this will only exacerbate the situation. These are Year 10 boys, and swearing is their normal way of communicating anger – there is no point in her making a big deal out of it. She needs to get the CD off the students quickly, because that will solve the problem temporarily – if she has the CD then she can decide what is done with it. If Patrick keeps the CD, it is likely that Colin will try to get it off him physically. Her tone is very clear and direct – she tells him to give it to her NOW, rather than asking him. She also separates the two boys, hoping that this will stop the argument immediately.

Unfortunately, the conflict resumes a few minutes later, and the teacher realizes that she must take further action to settle it. The boys swear at each other, and threaten physical violence. This is unacceptable, and the teacher removes them from the room to talk to them further. By doing this, she can deal with the problem away from the rest of the class. The class can get on with their work rather than watching her talk to the boys. Again, the teacher tells them very firmly that they *must* go outside – she will take no argument on this point.

Once outside, the teacher uses the CD as a tool for sanctioning the boys – if they do keep arguing she will pass it to the Head. She hopes that this threat will calm them down. She then deals with Patrick first – he is the less aggressive of the two and she has no real wish to punish him. After sending him back inside, she can deal with Colin in a more peaceful atmosphere. Unfortunately, Colin continues with his aggressive stance. The teacher is well aware of how easily Colin can be 'set off', and she maintains a very calm but firm manner with him. She points out to him what will happen if he does go ahead and hit Patrick. Then she allows Colin to tell his side of the story – by listening to him and taking his points seriously, she shows her human side, and she also shows that she is willing to believe and trust him.

Colin swears again, and again the teacher chooses to ignore it, but this time she issues a final warning. She then offers a solution, one that is deferred to break time, when she will have more opportunity to deal with the problem. She is aware that she needs to get back inside to her class now. Finally, she asks Colin to sit outside for the rest of the lesson, thus avoiding further possibility of physical confrontation. Notice how firm the teacher's tone has been in dealing with this whole situation, while at the same time remaining calm and non-confrontational. She *tells* them what to do, rather than asking them, thus maintaining a feeling that she is in control, no matter how nervous she feels inside. Notice too how she uses their names repeatedly, ensuring that she has their full attention when she is talking to them.

A bad example
Colin and Patrick are arguing about who owns a CD. Colin claims that he lent it to Patrick, but Patrick disagrees.

> Colin: Give it back, you ******!
> Patrick: Get real, Colin. It's mine. I never lent it to you.
> Miss Cook: Boys. Will you please stop arguing?
> Colin: He nicked my CD, miss.
> Patrick: He called me a ******, miss!
> Miss Cook: *[Sounding very irritated.]* Look, will you both stop using such foul language and get on with your work now. Do you want to be in detention with me after the lesson? No? Well, would you shut up then and get back to work.

The boys grudgingly settle to work, but a few minutes later they start arguing again.

> Colin: I'm gonna get you after school, you ****.
> Patrick: Oh yeah? Well I'm gonna mash your head right now your stupid ******!

The boys are on their feet, taking up threatening postures.

> Miss Cook: Right. Stop that now. Sit down.
> Colin: You ain't gonna mash my head you thick *******!
> Patrick: Oh yeah? Come on then, Colin. You think you're hard. *[He holds up his fists.]*
> Miss Cook: WILL YOU STOP IT AND SIT DOWN!!

It is too late, the boys are already fighting, and the rest of the class is urging them on. Miss Cook tries to get to them to separate them.

The Class: Fight! Fight! Fight! Fight!
Miss Cook: WILL YOU ALL STOP IT AND SIT DOWN
NOW!!

Commentary on the bad example

Notice how quickly the fight escalates here, because the teacher does not intervene firmly enough right at the beginning. Instead of *telling* them what she wants, she *asks* them to stop arguing. She also calls them 'boys', instead of addressing them by name, which lessens the impact of what she says. She threatens a detention as a way of solving the problem, rather than moving into the quarrel and removing the cause of friction, the CD. She also asks them to 'shut up', rather than telling them to 'be quiet'. By reflecting their own attitude in this way, and using an irritated tone, she is more likely to add to the conflict than to dissipate it.

After a few minutes the conflict is still there, and the boys start arguing again. Because the teacher did not intervene sufficiently early, it is now too late for her to stop a physical quarrel taking place. Again, she tells them to sit down rather than moving in to separate them or to take them outside, away from the class. But it is all too late – the fight is inevitable.

Serious verbal abuse

Age group: Year 8.
Details of the problem: Nina has a major problem with managing her anger, and when she does get annoyed, she lashes out verbally, swearing at anybody and everybody, including the head teacher!

A good example

The teacher sees Nina passing a cigarette to a friend during the lesson. He is tempted to ignore it, rather than start a confrontation, but Annie has spotted it and pipes up ...

Annie: Sir! I just saw Nina give Charlene a fag!
Nina: Shut ya face, ya boffin!
Charlene: Or we'll get ya after school!

Mr O'Gara: Nina. Charlene. Come here please. And bring your bags with you. *[He signals for them to come to his desk.]*

Nina: I ain't moving nowhere.

Mr O'Gara: I'll ask you again. Nina. Charlene. Come here now and bring your bags with you. That's your last warning.

Charlene: Come on, Nina. I don't wanna be in detention with the old goat. *[They go over to his desk.]*

Mr O'Gara: I'll pretend I didn't hear that. *[He stands up.]* Right. I'm going to give you one chance to hand me the cigarettes, nothing further said. Otherwise you're going to get in serious trouble, because I'll have to phone your parents and tell them about it.

Nina: I ain't givin' you my ∗∗∗∗∗∗∗ fags. And anyway, my parents know that I smoke. So there, you old ∗∗∗∗.

Mr O'Gara: Nina. Your language is appalling. And just because I'm an old goat, doesn't mean I won't be offended by it. *[The rest of the class laughs.]* Swear again and you're in detention. Now hand over the cigarettes. This is a one-time-only offer. Either hand them over or it has to go further.

Charlene: Can we have them back?

Mr O'Gara: Have what back? What are you admitting to having?

Charlene: Oh. I see. Nothing. Here you go, sir. *[She hands him the cigarette that Nina has given her.]*

Mr O'Gara: *[Crushing the cigarette and putting it in the bin.]* Thank you, Charlene, you may go and sit down. Nina? I want you to give me the rest of the packet.

Nina: No way, you ∗∗∗∗∗∗∗ ∗∗∗∗∗∗! They're mine!

Mr O'Gara: Right, Nina. You had your warning. That's a ten minute detention with me after the lesson. I want us to go outside the room and discuss this further, before you get in more serious trouble.

Nina: I ain't comin' to your ∗∗∗∗∗∗∗ detention. No ∗∗∗∗∗∗∗ way. And I ain't goin' outside the room with you, you ∗∗∗∗!

Mr O'Gara: Okay, then. Your detention has now gone up to twenty minutes and I'm going to have to speak to your head of year about your appalling language. You know that swearing is not allowed, Nina, and you are continuing to break that rule. Let's go outside and discuss this further, shall we?

He walks over to the door, leaving Nina standing at his desk. Eventually, she follows him outside. He closes the door behind them.

Mr O'Gara: Right, Nina. At the moment you have earned twenty minutes in detention with me. You know that cigarettes are not allowed in school, and neither is swearing. I want you to give me the packet of cigarettes now, please.

Nina: No. *[But she is starting to calm down.]*

Mr O'Gara: Look, Nina. You're forcing me to take this further. Is that what you really want?

Nina: No.

Mr O'Gara: Then hand me the cigarettes. Come on. Do it secretly so no one will see. I don't want the other teachers thinking that I'm getting fags off the kids, do I?

He smiles. Eventually Nina does too. They laugh as she hands over the packet surreptitiously.

Mr O'Gara: Right. Back inside. And don't let me catch you with fags again, eh, Nina?

Commentary on the good example

This is a very difficult situation to deal with. The students have cigarettes and this is clearly a serious breach of the rules. However, the teacher has to work with these students in the future, and he feels it is very important to develop a good relationship with them at this point. If he does deem it necessary to inform on them, he can do this at a later stage, after he has dealt with the incident. As soon as the problem starts, the teacher intervenes by telling the two girls to come to his desk. Fortunately, Charlene has more sense than Nina and realizes that the teacher is serious. She calls him an 'old goat', an insult that he deals with in a humorous way (see Chapter 4).

He offers the students a 'get-out clause' by saying that if they give him the cigarettes he will take the matter no further. Unfortunately, Nina immediately starts swearing at him. He deflects this by remaining calm and also gets a laugh from the class by referring to Charlene's insult. He warns Nina that if she swears again, she will be punished. He then deals with Charlene, the less confrontational student, who is willing to go along with his offer. Once Charlene has gone to sit back down, he can deal with Nina on an individual basis.

Regrettably, Nina swears again, and the teacher is forced to carry out the punishment that he has threatened. He also tells her that he will have to take the matter up with her head of year. He needs to get her away from the rest of the class so that she is removed from her audience. By walking over to the door, he leaves Nina stranded on her own, and she is forced to follow him rather than look stupid standing there at the front of the class. Once outside, the teacher manages to calm things down. Again, he uses humour, deflecting the tension by making a joke, and showing that he is human too. Happily, this time Nina goes along with what he wants.

Notice how, throughout the incident, the teacher remains calm and relaxed. When he is forced to sanction, he does so in a de-personalized, non-threatening way. Although this time the teacher has chosen to ignore the cigarettes, if he does catch the students with them again he will probably have to report them to a more senior member of staff. He hints at this in his final remark to Nina. By demonstrating that he knows many of the students do smoke, but explaining that he doesn't want to have any evidence of this, the teacher shows his human side.

A bad example
The teacher sees Nina passing a cigarette to a friend during the lesson. He is tempted to ignore it, rather than start a confrontation, but Annie has spotted it and pipes up . . .

Annie: Sir! I just saw Nina give Charlene a fag!
Nina: Shut ya face, ya boffin!
Charlene: Or we'll get ya after school!
Mr O'Gara: Girls. Can you stop being so rude? And can you give me the cigarettes? You know they're not allowed in school. You're both in detention with me after class. I'm going to have to phone your parents after school.
Charlene: That's not fair, sir! I didn't do anything!

Mr O'Gara: Oh do be quiet Charlene, and get on with your work.

Nina: You can phone my parents. They already know I smoke. And anyway, I don't care, you ****** ******!

Mr O'Gara: What did you call me?

Nina: A ****** ******!

Mr O'Gara: *[Shouting.]* Right, young lady! You're in trouble now! That's an hour's detention with me after class. Come over here and give me the cigarettes!

Nina: Get stuffed you ****!

Mr O'Gara: How dare you! *[He goes over to her.]* Give me those cigarettes now or else!

Nina: **** off! I ain't giving you my fags you old ****!

Mr O'Gara: *[Shouting in her face.]* Get out now! And don't come back!

Nina: *[Getting up and shouting back in his face.]* I'm telling my mum on you! You can't talk to me like that you ****** ******! *[She storms out.]*

Commentary on the bad example

This confrontation ends very differently from the first example, and it is unlikely that Nina and Mr O'Gara will be able to repair their relationship. It is also probable that Nina will now be in serious trouble. The first mistake that the teacher makes is to talk to the students across the class, from his desk, rather than getting them to come to him. He immediately sanctions them both and tells them that he will call their parents. When Charlene complains, he dismisses her out of hand.

Nina swears at him, and he makes the classic mistake of asking her '*What did you call me?*'. She, of course, is only too happy to repeat the insult! The teacher loses his cool and starts shouting at her, which is guaranteed to escalate the situation. Without warning, her detention is increased to an hour, and she is still expected to capitulate and give him the cigarettes.

Now the teacher moves into Nina's personal space, threatening her and shouting in her face. For a confrontational student, such an aggressive way of dealing with the issue in front of the whole class can mean only one thing – the student will explode right back at the teacher. Once again, she swears at him. When he sends her out, she leaves with a parting threat and a volley of abuse.

The dangerous object

Age group: Year 3.

Details of the problem: Rikky has been warned on previous occasions that he must not play around with scissors, and the class have talked about why they should not do this, and how unsafe it could be. However, Rikky still has a tendency to wave scissors around dangerously, and in the past he has cut the other children's hair and clothes with them.

A good example

Rikky has a pair of scissors and is threatening to cut Marilyn's hair with them. She has started crying.

Marilyn: Miss! Miss! Rikky's gonna cut my hair! Make him stop!

Rikky: I'm only playing, miss. I'm not really gonna cut her hair.

Miss Pirot: Marilyn, could you go and set out the drinks for break time? That's excellent, thanks very much Marilyn. *[Marilyn goes to sort out the drinks.]* Now, Rikky. I want you to give me those scissors right this minute. Hand them over. *[She holds out her hand.]*

Rikky: Oh, miss! That's not fair. I wasn't doing nothing with them. I need them to cut my maps out.

Miss Pirot: Rikky. Hand them to me right now please.

Rikky: *[Starting to get aggravated.]* No. I won't. I can't do my work without them.

Miss Pirot: *[Clapping her hands.]* Right! I'd like everybody to put down what they're doing and look at me. Looking at me and listening please!

The class put down their maps and their scissors and look at the teacher. She is now studiously ignoring Rikky.

Miss Pirot: Right! I'm going to set you all a challenge to see how clever you are. What I'd like you to do is to tear around your maps by hand, and I want to see who can do it best. The winner gets a gold star and a sticker of their choice! I'm going to time you – you have ten minutes to finish this work. Ready, steady, go.

When she looks back at Rikky, he has started tearing around his map by hand. She quickly picks up his scissors without him noticing.

Commentary on the good example

Once again, the teacher's early intervention is crucial in preventing a more serious situation from developing. If she had left Rikky to his own devices, he might well have actually cut Marilyn by accident. The teacher's first step is to remove Marilyn from the equation, by offering her an exciting alternative. This will also help distract Marilyn from being upset. Next, she demands that Rikky hand over the scissors. His response, that he needs them for his work, is in fact quite true. When she realizes that he might become confrontational if she continues, the teacher quickly decides to take a different tack.

At this age, children are relatively easy to distract, and this is what the teacher decides to do. She ignores Rikky, removing her attention from him, and getting the class's attention instead. She then offers them a challenge that means they won't have to use the scissors at all. She 'sweetens' the contest with a reward that she knows Rikky likes – a gold star and a sticker. By the time she looks back at Rikky, he is engrossed in the challenge and she can subtly remove the dangerous object from his table.

A bad example

Rikky has a pair of scissors and is threatening to cut Marilyn's hair with them. She has started crying.

Marilyn: Miss! Miss! Rikky's gonna cut my hair! Make him stop!

Rikky: I'm only playing, miss. I'm not really gonna cut her hair.

Miss Pirot: Rikky. I've asked you before and I'll ask you again. Can you please stop playing with the scissors? You know it's dangerous. Marilyn, do stop being silly and crying like that. He hasn't hurt you, has he?

Rikky: Oh, miss! That's not fair. I wasn't doing nothing with them. I need them to cut my maps out.

Miss Pirot: Can you hand me the scissors now, Rikky, or I won't let you do the activity.

Rikky: *[Starting to get aggravated.]* No. That's not fair. I won't. I can't do my work without them.

Miss Pirot: *[Shouting.]* Rikky! Give me the scissors or there's no play time for you today!

Now both Rikky and Marilyn are crying. The rest of the class have stopped working to watch.

Miss Pirot: Now look what you've done, you silly children! Do shut up and get on with the work!

Rikky: I hate you!

Miss Pirot: And I hate you, Rikky! Leave the room now and go to stand outside the Head's office. *[Exasperated.]* Oh, Marilyn, do stop crying!

Commentary on the bad example

This time, instead of removing Marilyn from the situation, the teacher accuses her of being silly, rather an unfair charge! When Rikky refuses to comply with her, the teacher quickly becomes annoyed and starts to shout, rather than remaining calm and dealing with the problem in a rational way. She threatens Rikky without warning, that he will lose his play time, rather than taking his complaint seriously, that he cannot do the work without the scissors. When the rest of the class start to watch the incident, she calls both Rikky and Marilyn 'silly' and tells them to 'shut up'. This rudeness is bound to aggravate things, and Rikky responds by telling her he 'hates her'. She reacts rudely again, and the situation is only 'resolved' by sending him to the Head's office, rather an over-reaction to a problem that should have been easily dealt with. She is left with a class who are completely distracted from their work, and a student who is in floods of tears.

Part Six

If All Else Fails . . .

14 I can't cope anymore!

Teaching is an extremely difficult profession to work in. It is emotionally, physically and psychologically taxing, and there will be times when you do feel as though you just can't cope anymore. No matter how hard you try, you may believe that you are making no headway in improving the behaviour of your students. This can be extremely demoralizing. Day after day, you arrive at your job, knowing that you must face students who simply will not behave for you. You might begin to dread coming into work, knowing that you will have to face such a difficult day. At these times, it is important to differentiate between the inevitable ups and downs of a teaching career, and the signs of a more major problem. In this chapter we will be looking at how you can identify exactly what the problem is, and some of the options you have for dealing with it.

What is the problem?

The feeling that you can't cope anymore can build up slowly, or it can arrive without warning one day when you feel that you simply can't get out of bed and go into work. Sometimes, the problem is a temporary one, and one that can be dealt with relatively easily. On the other hand, it could be a more long-term issue, and one that will require more extreme measures to solve. Here are some thoughts about exactly what the problem might be.

Seasonal effects

The time of the year can have a huge impact on your ability to cope with bad behaviour. At the start of the year, you will be full of energy, ready to deal with whatever the students can throw at you. Of course, this is the time of year when you need this extra energy the most. It is extremely stressful to be meeting large numbers of new people, trying to learn names, and, if you are new at your school, finding your way around the building, the systems, and so on.

Towards the end of the first term, energy levels fall low, the nights become darker and the students more fractious. Ask yourself – is the feeling that I can't cope a symptom of general tiredness? Will things seem better at the beginning of a new term, when I've had a holiday and I feel refreshed and ready to face my students again? If this is the case, try to organize yourself a proper break from teaching during your holidays. Refuse to take any planning or marking home with you, book yourself a flight to somewhere sunny, and concentrate on recharging your batteries, ready to plunge in with renewed vigour when you return to school next term.

Overwork

It could be that you are becoming excessively tired because you are overworked. If you do take on too much, this can lead to problems dealing with your actual classroom teaching. You may have other commitments, either inside or outside of school, that cause you additional stress and leave you too exhausted to deal properly with the behaviour management of your classes. Think very carefully about your extra curricular responsibilities. Although these can offer a welcome change from classroom teaching, and a good opportunity to get to know your students on a one-to-one level, they also mean that you have to stay late after a full working day. Your number one priority has to be your health and sanity – learn to say 'no' to demands on your time!

The school

On the other hand, it could be the school itself that is the problem. In Chapter 11 we explored some of the ways that the school can impact on behaviour in the classroom. Are your school buildings run down and uncared for? Is the whole school ethos a negative and confrontational one? Is there poor continuity of staff and a management that fails to support you? And is the whole school behaviour policy ineffective in dealing with the issues that you face? If you have answered 'yes' to some of these questions, then it is likely that the school you are working at has problems with controlling its students.

If this is the situation you are in, make sure you turn to other staff for support. Again, there is information about this in Chapter 11. And if you feel that your personal situation is getting out of hand, and that you alone cannot even start to improve things at your school, then you will need to decide whether you are willing to stay. As I have said, the most important thing at the end of the day is for you to stay healthy and happy!

What are the danger signs?

A certain amount and type of stress is healthy, because it is essential in keeping us energetic and 'alive'. We all need a certain level of stimulation if we are not to become dissatisfied with our work. After all, you probably came into teaching because you would have been bored by an office job! Teaching offers us many different challenges, and it can be the most wonderful career in the world. On the other hand, a difficult teaching job can be too much for some people to cope with, and there is no shame at all attached to feeling that you cannot cope.

Stress is a response to a difficult situation, and when we are stressed we produce high levels of adrenaline which can result in certain physical and emotional symptoms. Originally, the production of adrenaline helped us in a 'fight or flight' situation, where our ancestors needed to be ready to flee from danger or to wrestle the proverbial mammoth to the ground. The problem in our modern world is that we become overstressed, producing all this adrenaline, without any means of using it up. As a teacher, you have to stay and deal with the stressful circumstances, rather than running away or resorting to physical ways of solving it. And if your school situation is problematic, and your stress levels are too high, your health could be put at risk, and not even the most wonderful career in the world is worth that! The symptoms of stress vary according to the individual, but there are some common signs that you could look out for to check whether you are becoming stressed by your work:

- *Physical Symptoms*
  - *Difficulty sleeping:* If you are having difficulty sleeping, particularly on a Sunday night when you are preparing for the week ahead, you could well be experiencing high

levels of stress connected with your work. Do you dream about your problem classes? And do your dreams become nightmares in which you can no longer cope?

— *Feeling sick:* That hollow feeling in the pit of the stomach is, I am sure, something that many teachers can relate to, and certainly all those who have worked in a difficult school. Do you feel sick when you are about to face your most difficult class, or classes? Or do you have that sick feeling all the time? If you do, it is highly likely that you are suffering from excessive stress.

— *Increased heart rate:* In addition to feeling sick, you might find that your heart begins to beat faster because of the production of adrenaline. Does this happen to you when you are about to teach? Again, a raised heart rate is a symptom of stress.

— *Sweaty palms:* If your palms become sweaty in a tense situation, this could be a further sign that you are over-stressed.

- *Emotional Symptoms*
  - *Loss of confidence:* When you feel that you can't cope with the behaviour of your students, it is all too easy to lose confidence in your teaching abilities. Your perception of what is actually happening in your classroom can become distorted, and the problems you are experiencing might loom much larger than they are in reality.
  - *Becoming defensive:* In addition to losing confidence in yourself, you might also find that you become overly defensive, expecting the worst from your students. As we have seen, this can be extremely counter-productive and can lead to an even more stressful situation.
  - *Bursting into tears:* All too often, I have seen teachers reduced to tears in the staffroom, or even in the class-room. What other job forces this sort of humiliation on its workers? If you do find yourself feeling overly vulner-able and emotional, this could well be a sign of very high stress levels.
  - *Becoming snappy:* When you or your colleagues are stressed, the temptation to snap at each other becomes greater, particularly if you are all dealing with similarly

difficult students. Again, poor relationships between the staff in a school can indicate a time of high stress, perhaps during an inspection or even on an everyday basis.

How do you cope?

How, then, do you cope if your stress levels are high, and you feel that behaviour management problems are getting on top of you? First, follow the advice given in this book. Many of the tips that I have given are simple to put in place, but will make a huge difference to behaviour in your classes. Here are a few other thoughts that might help you, when you find yourself becoming stressed:

Use your support systems
In my experience, teachers are wonderful at supporting their colleagues. As I said in Chapter 11, use all the support systems that are available to you. Talk about your problems with someone sympathetic – sometimes all that you need is a shoulder to cry on, or a caring ear in which to pour out your woes. Why not ask to watch another teacher's classes, someone who you know has excellent classroom control? Although this is usually an option available only to newly qualified teachers, a supportive head might allow you to do this too if you explain how bad you are feeling. By watching how someone else copes with similar students to your own, you will pick up some useful tips that you can utilize in your own classroom.

Keep a perspective
In a difficult school it is sometimes hard to keep a perspective on what you are really achieving. A major problem is that you never get to see the students in their other classes, and so you have no real idea of how they behave for their other teachers. Always remember, a badly behaved class is not necessarily a reflection of your talents as a teacher, but is a manifestation of many other contributing factors. Remember, too, that at the end of the day the world really is not going to end if your students won't behave themselves. Try to avoid blowing up incidents of poor behaviour into more than they really are.

React from the head

This tip, explained fully in Chapter 3, is very useful when you are feeling that you can't cope anymore. An intellectual response, rather than an emotional one, will lower your stress levels and increase your ability to deal with the problems that do arise. Teaching is an emotional job and we often invest a great deal of emotional energy in it. Make sure your rational intellect keeps the upper hand!

Take heart from small successes

When you are feeling at your most depressed, take a look at your classes to see what small steps they have taken that you can be proud of. For a teacher in a difficult school, or working with a difficult class, a small step such as getting your students to stay in their chairs may represent a huge achievement. Praise and reward *yourself* for these achievements, as well as your students. There are many people who could not even start to make the progress you have made! Take a look at what your good students are achieving as well – often when we are dealing with generally poor behaviour it becomes easy to overlook the work of our well-behaved children.

Don't be a perfectionist

Remember, too, not to be a perfectionist. If a student does choose to opt out of your lessons, or out of the education system as a whole, try your best, but don't beat yourself up about it. As long as you are doing the best that you can for your children, then you are doing your job. If a lesson does go wrong, accept that you are human, and that you will make mistakes. There is no point in dwelling on what is past and gone – look to the future, learn from the errors you make, and with time things will improve. Honestly!

Take time out

There is no shame in sometimes making life easy for yourself, particularly if you are dealing with difficult children on a daily basis. On occasions, give yourself a break, by showing a video, or going to the computer room. Look at the section on lessons that are 'Guaranteed to succeed' in Chapter 6 for some more ideas about how you might give yourself a lesson off.

Take time off

If you are suffering from high stress levels, do go to see your doctor. It could be that you need to take some time off sick to recover. Again, you should not be embarrassed or ashamed if you do need to take sick leave. Teaching is an extremely taxing profession, and you will not be able to work at your best if you are tense and stressed. Above all, make your own health your first priority!

Get out!?

At some stage, you might want to ask yourself whether you are actually willing to cope anymore with your school, or with teaching as a profession. This is a personal decision that only you can take, but one that you will obviously want to consider long and carefully. If could be that you have become disillusioned with your current school, but that changing to a job somewhere else will refresh your outlook on teaching as a career. Only you can decide!

Whether you do decide to change jobs, or change careers, I wish you all the best in your future. And please don't forget, teachers make a huge difference to the lives of all their students. There are so many good children out there who need your talents and your help. And your badly behaved students are in desperate need of your care and attention to help them succeed, no matter how much they might mistreat you. So, follow the advice in this book, keep plugging away, and I promise you that you *will* be successful in 'getting the buggers to behave'!

Index